Bat, Bowl and Beyond: The Essential Book for New Players and Cricket Fans.

From First Swing to Full Knowledge.

by S. A. Carmody

KMCS Publishing

Bat, Bowl and Beyond
© 2025 Sarah A. Carmody
Published by KMCS Publishing

All rights reserved. No part of this publication may be reproduced, stored in a retrieval system or transmitted in any form or by any means, electronic, mechanical, photocopying, recording or otherwise, without the prior written permission of the publisher, except for brief quotations used in reviews or scholarly works.

ISBN 978-1-918259-15-5 (paperback)
ISBN 978-1-918259-16-2 (ebook)

First published in the United Kingdom by KMCS Publishing.

This book is intended for general information. Every effort has been made to ensure accuracy at the time of writing, although cricket is an evolving sport and laws and guidance may change. Some information may therefore differ from the most current versions published after the manuscript deadline. Readers should consult the latest official updates from the MCC, ECB or relevant governing bodies for the newest information.

The foreword by the President of Yorkshire County Cricket Club is a personal contribution. Yorkshire County Cricket Club has not reviewed or officially endorsed this publication.

Printed in the United Kingdom.

Dedication

To all those who keep the grassroots cricket clubs in our country going, the volunteers, coaches, players, and supporters who make the game possible week after week.

Especially to Paul Berry, Chairman of St Chad's Broomfield Cricket Club in Leeds, whose countless hours of groundwork and tireless oversight of senior teams (both men and women), junior teams (both girls and boys), and senior and junior games is nothing short of incredible. Your commitment keeps the heart of cricket beating strong.

FOREWORD BY DR JANE POWELL-PRESIDENT OF YORKSHIRE COUNTY CRICKET CLUB.

When I first picked up a bat as a young girl, I never imagined the journey cricket would take me on, from playing for England to becoming the first female President of Yorkshire County Cricket Club. It's been a path filled with challenges, triumphs, and above all, a deep love for the game. So, when Sarah Carmody asked me to write this foreword, I felt genuinely honoured.

Bat, Bowl and Beyond is a book that speaks to the heart of cricket, not just the rules and techniques, but the spirit, the people, and the possibilities. Sarah's story is extraordinary. In just four years, she's gone from newcomer to advocate, coach, and now cricket author. Her passion is infectious, and her commitment to making cricket inclusive and accessible is something I deeply admire.

Reading this book reminded me of why I fell in love with the game. Sarah captures the joy of a young team facing giants with courage, the excitement of discovering new formats like blind cricket, and the importance of creating spaces where everyone, regardless of age, gender, or ability, can belong. Her spotlight on disability cricket and her thoughtful approach to representation make this book not only informative but truly inspiring.

Whether you're picking up a bat for the first time or have been part of the cricketing world for decades, *Bat, Bowl and Beyond* offers something special. It's a celebration of what cricket is and what it can become.

I'm proud to support this book and the incredible work Sarah is doing. The game is better for having her in it.

Jane Powell
President, Yorkshire County Cricket Club
Former Captain, England Women's Cricket Team

INTRODUCTION

I came to cricket later than most. When I first put on pads and picked up a bat in January 2022, I was completely new to the sport, curious but unsure, and often overwhelmed by how much there was to learn. This book grew out of those early weeks and months. I have included the many things I wished I had known at the start, from the most basic questions to the details that only begin to make sense once you have stood on a boundary in the cold wondering whether you are in the right place.

In 2023, I completed my Level 2 Core Coaching Course with Yorkshire's legendary Kev Gresham. His mixture of deep knowledge and sharp humour makes him an unforgettable teacher. He increases the love of the game simply by being in the room, and I am grateful for everything he taught me.

I was also inspired by Dr Jane Powell, the first female President of Yorkshire. Her leadership within the game, her achievements, and her generosity of spirit continue to encourage so many of us. I was overjoyed when she agreed to write the foreword for this book.

Coaching children has become one of the greatest joys of my life. I love helping girls discover cricket for the first time, watching them build confidence, form teams, create friendships and find their own place in the sport. The game has taught me far more than rules, field positions and techniques. Cricket is a community, a grass-roots miracle built on volunteers, patience, teamwork and the belief that everyone deserves a chance. Beyond the pitch, I do not think anything has taught me more about people and human nature.

This book is for everyone. It is for absolute beginners who want to understand the basics and for seasoned experts who enjoy looking at the sport from a fresh angle. Any mistakes are entirely mine. I am still learning and will continue to learn as long as I am lucky enough to be part of this remarkable game.

- S. A. Carmody

CONTENTS

Introduction

PART ONE.

Chapter One. Who is Cricket For?

Chapter Two. How to get Involved in Cricket.

Chapter Three. The Structure of a Grassroots Cricket Club.

Chapter Four. Getting to Know Cricket.

Chapter Five: Understanding the Game.

Chapter Six. Innings and Overs.

Chapter Seven: How to Score Runs.

Chapter Eight: Getting Out: All the Ways to be Dismissed.

Chapter Nine: Bowling Style and Deliveries

Chapter Ten: Batting Strokes: From Defence to Reverse Sweep.

Chapter Eleven: Fielding Explained.

Chapter Twelve: Umpires, Signals, and Decisions.

Chapter Thirteen: Staying Safe: Protective Gear and Injury Prevention.

Chapter Fourteen: Practising and Nets.

Chapter Fifteen: Match Day: What to Expect.

Chapter Sixteen: Cricket Etiquette and Spirit of the Game.

Chapter Seventeen: Cricket Superstitions from Grassroots and Beyond.

Chapter Eighteen: Cricket Slang and What it Means.

Chapter Nineteen: The Cricket Dictionary (A-Z).

Chapter Twenty: Who Said That? Famous Cricket Quotes.

PART TWO

Chapter Twenty-One: Cricket. From Humble Beginnings to Modern Day.

Chapter Twenty-Two: The History of Men's Cricket.

Chapter Twenty-Three: The History of Women's Cricket.

Chapter Twenty-Four: Disability Cricket and its Pioneers.

PART THREE

Chapter Twenty-Five: The History of the Laws of Cricket.

Chapter Twenty-Six: The History of Scoring.

Chapter Twenty-Seven The History of the Cricket Bat.

Chapter Twenty-Eight The History of Wickets.

Chapter Twenty-Nine: The History of the Cricket Ball.

PART FOUR

Chapter Thirty: Groundstaff: The Hidden Force in Cricket.

Chapter Thirty-One: The Barmy Army.

Chapter Thirty-Two: Red Ball v White Ball v Pink Ball in Cricket.

Chapter Thirty-Three: The Story of the Test Match.

Chapter Thirty-Four: The World Test Championship.

Chapter Thirty-Five The Twenty20 Competition.

Chapter Thirty-Six The Hundred Competition.

Chapter Thirty-Seven: The County Championship.

PART FIVE

Chapter Thirty-Eight: The Marylebone Cricket Club (MCC).

Chapter Thirty-Nine: The International Cricket Council (ICC).

Chapter Forty: The England and Wales Cricket Board (ECB).

Chapter Forty-One: The Lord's Taverners.

Chapter Forty-Two: County Cricket Boards.

Chapter Forty-Three: County Cricket Clubs.

Chapter Forty-Four: Conclusion-The Endless Story of Cricket.

Acknowledgements

Bibliography and References

Further Reading

CHAPTER ONE: WHO IS CRICKET FOR?

Cricket is a game for everyone, no matter your age, gender, background, or ability.

It's played by:

. **Women** – from grassroots club teams to international stars.

. **Men** – at every level, from village greens to professional stadiums.

. **Girls and Boys** – in schools, clubs, and back-gardens all over the world.

. **People with Disabilities** – including blind cricket, deaf cricket, cricket for wheelchair users, and learning disability cricket.

Cricket is one of the most inclusive sports in the world. Whatever your skill level or experience, there's a team and a format that's right for you. You just need enthusiasm, a willingness to learn, and a love for being part of a team.

Everyone belongs in cricket.

CHAPTER TWO: HOW TO GET INVOLVED IN CRICKET

For Children – All Stars and Dynamos

All Stars Cricket (ages 5–8):

. A fun, safe introduction to cricket.

. Focuses on simple skills like catching, throwing, and hitting.

. Every child gets a personalised shirt, bat, and ball to keep.

Dynamos Cricket (ages 8–11):

. Builds on All Stars skills with more game-like activities.

. Great for kids ready to learn match rules and teamwork.

. Fun, fast-paced sessions designed to keep children active and confident.

. You can find both programmes through the ECB (England and Wales Cricket Board) website, just enter your postcode to see nearby sessions.

For Adults – Starting Cricket

Join a Local Club:

. Most clubs welcome beginners of all abilities, including complete newcomers.

. You don't need your own kit to start; many clubs will lend you equipment.

Soft Ball Cricket:

. Many clubs run soft ball cricket sessions for adults who want to learn without the fear of a hard ball.

. Great for fitness, socialising, and building confidence before moving to hard ball cricket.

. Search online for "cricket club near me" or check your county cricket board's website for a list of local clubs.

Top Tips for Getting Started

. Go along to watch a session first to see what it's like.

. Bring comfortable sports clothing and trainers.

. Don't be nervous. Cricket clubs are usually friendly, community-focused places that welcome new faces.

From Backyards to Boundaries – Cricketers' Recollections of Their First Steps

Every international superstar, before the packed stadiums and TV cameras, was once a child holding a bat too big for their hands or bowling with a tennis ball in the street. These are their stories of backyards and beaches, borrowed bats and makeshift wickets, of nervous first club games and the sparks that lit lifelong passions.

England – Backyard Battles and County Dreams

Ben Stokes
Growing up in New Zealand before moving to Cumbria, Stokes recalls hours spent in the backyard with his dad, former rugby league professional Ged Stokes. He'd hurl tennis balls at young Ben with unrelenting pace, teaching him toughness. Stokes

often says those bruising backyard contests taught him to "never back down," a quality that became his hallmark.

Joe Root
Root's story begins in Sheffield, where he and his brother Billy (who also became a professional) would use the family driveway as their pitch. Their dad umpired, Mum provided drinks, and the neighbours learned patience as windows occasionally shattered. Joe would mimic his hero Michael Vaughan, practising cover drives for hours until the ball rolled smooth over the tarmac.

Charlotte Edwards
The former England women's captain often tells of how she played endless matches with her brothers in the back garden in Huntingdon. She was "always the last one out," refusing to give up the bat. By 12, she had made her county debut for Huntingdonshire boys' under-15s, still wearing her school uniform skirt because she didn't own cricket whites.

India – Streets, Maidens, and Tennis Balls

Sachin Tendulkar
Tendulkar's cricketing origin is legendary. As a boy in Mumbai, he was given his first bat by his elder brother, who recognised his restless energy. Sachin would practise in the cramped housing colonies of Bandra, using rubber balls and improvised stumps. His coach Ramakant Achrekar famously placed a one-rupee coin on the stumps; if bowlers dismissed him, they got the coin. If not, Sachin kept it. He still calls those coins "the best prizes of my life."

Mithali Raj
Mithali never wanted to play cricket; she dreamed of becoming a classical dancer. But when accompanying her brother to training in Hyderabad, she was asked to join in. Her natural timing stunned the coaches. By 16, she was making her India debut and scoring a century. She later said, "If not for tagging along with my brother, I might never have picked up a bat."

Virat Kohli
In Delhi, Kohli's first memories are of his father waking him at 5am for academy practice. Kohli would cry about the early mornings, but his dad insisted on discipline. Virat later said his father's sacrifices, especially driving him across the city after long

workdays, gave him the hunger to succeed after his father's death when Virat was just 18.

Australia – Beaches, Backyards, and Nets in the Heat

Don Bradman
Before he became "The Don," young Bradman honed his skills with a stump and a golf ball against a water tank in Bowral. The tank's curved surface made the ball shoot off unpredictably, sharpening his reflexes. Bradman said those hours alone were the foundation of his near-mythical batting.

Ellyse Perry
Australia's superstar all-rounder was a natural at *every* sport. She played backyard cricket with her brother in Sydney, hitting balls over fences and then spending more time fetching them than batting. Perry became the youngest Australian, male or female, to play international cricket at just sixteen. Looking back, she laughs that, "I never imagined it would be cricket, not football, that chose me."

Shane Warne
Warne's first love was actually Aussie Rules football. But as a boy in suburban Melbourne, he also bowled endless leg-spin in the nets, copying the greats he watched on TV. He recalled how as a teenager, coaches told him he was "too unorthodox." Warne ignored them and changed cricket forever.

West Indies – Cricket on the Beaches

Brian Lara
In Trinidad, Lara's first bat was often a piece of wood, and matches on the street would run late into the evening. Lara's father enrolled him in the famous Harvard Coaching Clinic at just six-years-old, where his precocious talent was obvious. Neighbours still recall little Brian "owning" the cul-de-sac with his drives.

Stafanie Taylor
Growing up in Jamaica, Taylor's earliest cricket was played with boys on the street. She says she learned resilience by being the only girl: "If you got out, there was no second chance." Those battles toughened her up, making her one of the greatest all-rounders in women's cricket.

Pakistan & Sri Lanka – Tape Balls and Street Rivalries

Wasim Akram
Pakistan's "Sultan of Swing" first learned cricket with a tennis ball taped on one side, the classic Pakistani invention that mimics swing. He didn't play serious organised cricket until eighteen, yet his natural pace and skill were honed in those street games where every over was a challenge.

Sanath Jayasuriya
The Sri Lankan dasher grew up in Matara, playing barefoot cricket on beaches and dusty grounds. His fearless attacking style, charging bowlers, hitting on the up, was born out of needing to dominate in rough conditions with poor equipment.

South Africa & Beyond

Jonty Rhodes
Before he became the symbol of modern fielding, Jonty played endless backyard cricket in Pietermaritzburg. He was a multi-sport star, but he says cricket "was the only one where diving in the dirt was actually encouraged."

Shabnim Ismail (South Africa)
Known as the fastest bowler in women's cricket, Ismail grew up in the streets of Cape Town bowling to boys, often barefoot, with nothing but determination. She remembers the neighbours complaining when balls smashed into windows, but she also remembers thinking: *this is what I was born to do.*

These stories continue to matter because they highlight:

. **Accessibility** – Most started with little: tennis balls, garden pitches, or makeshift bats.

. **Family & Community** – Parents, siblings, or neighbours played key roles in encouraging them.

. **Character** – Early setbacks, teasing, or makeshift conditions, which built resilience and creativity.

. **Universality** – Whether in Sheffield, Mumbai, or Kingston, cricket's entry point was the same; joy, play, and belonging.

Every great innings, every five-fer, every trophy, has its roots in these small, almost throwaway moments: a child swinging at shadows in the garden, a taped-up tennis ball curving past a neighbour's gate, a father driving across a city at dawn. From these humble beginnings, cricket's greatest legends were born.

CHAPTER THREE: THE STRUCTURE OF A GRASSROOTS CRICKET CLUB

A grassroots cricket club is much more than just a cricket team; it's a whole community working together to keep the game alive. Most clubs are run almost entirely by volunteers, with a mix of formal roles and informal helpers.

Key Roles and Responsibilities

1. Chair

. The leader of the club.

. Oversees everything from cricket decisions to finances and facilities.

. Represents the club at local league meetings and in the wider cricket community.

2. Management Committee

A group of volunteers who make key decisions and help run the club. This usually includes:

. **Secretary** – handles administration, meeting minutes, and communication.

. **Treasurer** – manages the club's money.

. **Fixtures Secretary** – arranges matches with other clubs.

. **Safeguarding Officer** – ensures the club is safe for children and adults.

. **Membership Secretary** – keeps track of members and subscriptions.

. **Other Officers such as the Equality, Diversity, and Inclusion (EDI) Officer.**

3. Coaches

- Lead training sessions for juniors and seniors.
- Help players improve skills, fitness, and understanding of the game.
- Often volunteer parents or qualified England & Wales Cricket Board (ECB) coaches.

4. Captains & Team Managers

- Organise teams for matches.
- Make tactical decisions on match day.
- Keep team morale high and represent players' views to the committee.

5. Groundskeeper

- Maintains the pitch and outfield so matches can be played safely.
- Prepares wickets, marks lines, and ensures the playing area is in good condition.

6. Volunteers & Helpers

- Cover all the essential jobs like:
- Scoring matches
- Umpiring
- Running fundraising events
- Selling raffle tickets

7. The Tea-Maker

. A much-loved role in UK cricket!

. Prepares the famous cricket tea. Sandwiches, cakes, biscuits, fruit, and tea/coffee for players and officials at the interval.

8. The Bar

. Often run by volunteers or a rota of club members.

. Provides drinks and snacks after matches, helping raise money for the club.

The Wider Club Community

. **Family and Friends** – support players, watch games, and help with events.

. **Sponsors** – local businesses who contribute money or equipment in return for advertising.

. **Social Members** – people who don't play but enjoy being part of the club's social side.

. **Youth Players** – the future of the club, often starting in junior programmes like All Stars or Dynamos and staying on as part of the club's junior section.

Why It Works

A grassroots cricket club thrives because *everyone chips in*. It's about more than winning matches; it's about creating a welcoming space for people to play, watch, and enjoy cricket together.

From Village Greens to Glory – Famous Cricketers Remember Their Grassroots Clubs

Before they filled stadiums and signed autographs, the game's greats queued up for club teas, searched for lost balls in hedges, and played under leaky pavilion roofs. Grassroots cricket isn't just a pathway; it's the heartbeat of the sport. Many international stars never forgot the smells, sights, and quirks of their first clubs.

England – The Village Green Tradition

Alastair Cook – Wickham Bishops Cricket Club
England's record Test run-scorer often mentions Wickham Bishops CC in Essex, where he first played competitive club cricket. He remembers nervously turning out in borrowed whites, eating his first cricket tea (jam sandwiches and crisps), and realising the game was as much about friendships as runs. "It felt like the centre of the world," Cook later said.

Heather Knight – Plymstock Cricket Club
Before captaining England to World Cup glory, Knight cut her teeth at Plymstock CC in Devon. She talks fondly about long car journeys to matches with her dad, her early teammates cheering when she scored a single, and how older club members encouraged her to stick with the sport. "That little club gave me confidence that I belonged in cricket," she recalls.

Ben Stokes – Cockermouth Cricket Club
Stokes' local club in Cumbria became his English cricketing home after emigrating from New Zealand. He remembers being treated "like family" by the club, who saw his raw talent early. To this day, Cockermouth CC proudly display photos and shirts of their most famous alumnus, and Stokes makes a point of dropping by when he's home.

India – Maidens to Clubhouses

Rahul Dravid – St Joseph's Boys' High School & KSCA Leagues
Dravid first made his name in organised cricket with school and local club teams in Bangalore. He recalls the Karnataka State Cricket Association matches where he

would walk to the ground with his kitbag and queue for his chance. "Those games taught me patience, sometimes waiting all day to bat, only to be out for a duck," Dravid said.

Smriti Mandhana – Sangli Club Cricket
Growing up in Sangli, Maharashtra, Mandhana's entry into organised cricket was with boys' club teams. She still laughs about being sledged by older boys until she smashed them to the boundary. "Those early club games toughened me up. They didn't care I was a girl, and that was the best thing for me."

Australia – Community Clubs Under the Sun

Steve Smith – Menai Cricket Club
Smith began with Menai CC in Sydney's Sutherland Shire. His grassroots memories include carrying drinks as 12th man, long Saturdays scorched under the sun, and older players teasing him for his unusual batting stance. "Menai gave me the freedom to bat my way," Smith has said, a freedom that later redefined Test cricket.

Ellyse Perry – Beecroft Cricket Club
Before she was an international all-rounder, Perry played junior cricket at Beecroft CC in Sydney. She fondly recalls parents scoring matches, kids chasing balls into creeks, and post-match sausage sizzles. For Perry, those club days showed her cricket was a community, not just a game.

West Indies – Clubs with Carnival Spirit

Brian Lara – Harvard Cricket Club, Trinidad
Lara joined the prestigious Harvard CC at just 14. He remembers the nerves of walking into a senior dressing room full of big characters. "I just wanted to listen, absorb, and not get shouted at for dropping a catch." Harvard CC became his cricketing family, and even as a superstar he would return to train with them.

Stafanie Taylor – Boys' Club in Kingston
Taylor's earliest club games were for boys' teams in Kingston, Jamaica. She recalls the thrill of her first selection, and the confusion when she turned up and the opposition thought she was just a scorer or substitute. After a few cover drives, no one questioned her place again.

Pakistan & Sri Lanka – Clubs as Gateways

Inzamam-ul-Haq – Multan Cricket Club
Before Pakistan stardom, Inzamam played on the dusty grounds of Multan CC. He often spoke about matches where cows wandered across the outfield, or balls had to be dried after falling into irrigation ditches. "It wasn't glamorous, but it was cricket, and that was enough."

Chamari Athapaththu – Chilaw Marians CC
Sri Lanka's women's captain began her career at Chilaw Marians, one of the country's few clubs actively encouraging women's cricket. She remembers being "terrified" in her first senior club match, but older teammates rallied around her, making her feel at home.

South Africa – Clubs That Built Characters

AB de Villiers – Affies and Pretoria Cricket Club
De Villiers' memories of grassroots cricket are filled with school and local club matches where he and friends played all day before collapsing into exhausted heaps. "We just wanted to play until it was too dark to see," he says. His first Pretoria CC appearances were, in his words, "where cricket became life."

Mignon du Preez – Highveld Clubs
South Africa's long-time women's skipper played for small clubs around Pretoria and recalls how rare it was to see other girls playing. "I had to prove myself constantly, but those clubs gave me the confidence that I could be more than just a novelty."

Why Grassroots Memories Matter

. **Community Spirit** – Clubs made future stars feel part of something bigger.

. **Funny Firsts** – Wrong kit, cows on outfields, tea disasters, and being underestimated.

. **Role of Volunteers** – Parents, umpires, and scorers who kept the game alive.

. **Pride and Belonging** – Every player carried their club's badge long after moving to international fame.

A late summer match at St Chad's Broomfield CC, Headingley, Leeds

From Cockermouth to Kingston, Beecroft to Bangalore, the stories are the same: nervous debuts, borrowed whites, teammates who became family. Clubs weren't just stepping stones; they were homes, the places where legends first believed they belonged to the game.

CHAPTER FOUR: GETTING TO KNOW CRICKET

1. Why Cricket Can Seem Confusing (and Why You'll Love It)

Cricket has centuries of history and plenty of jargon. Underneath it all is a simple contest: one team scores runs; the other tries to stop them and take wickets. Once you grasp that, the rest is a matter of learning the language.

2. The Basics – What Cricket Actually Is

Two teams of eleven; one bats while the other bowls/fields, then they swap. Two batters are in at any time. Bowlers deliver in overs of six legal balls. The team with the most runs wins.

3. The Playing Area – Pitch, Crease, and Boundary

The pitch is a 22-yard strip with 'creases' marking where batters stand and bowlers must release. The boundary marks the edge of the field.

4. Clothing & Kit – What to Wear and Why

Whites for traditional formats, coloured kits for limited overs. Shoes: spikes for outdoors; rubber for indoors. Protective kit includes: helmet, gloves, pads, and abdo guard (box).

5. Your First Cricket Bat – Choosing the Right One

Pick size by height (kids 1–6 then Harrow; adults Short Handle unless 6'3 +). Choose a weight you can control. English willow = premium; Kashmir willow = durable and affordable. Feel matters most.

6. The Ball – What to Expect

Hard leather balls in matches (red, white, pink or orange). Start with soft or tennis balls for practice to build confidence and reduce risk.

7. Meet the Team – Roles and Positions

Batters score, bowlers take wickets, wicketkeepers catch behind the stumps, fielders save runs. All-rounders do both batting and bowling, the captain sets tactics.

Quick Facts:

> Teams: 2 teams of 11 players each.
>
> Objective: Score more runs than the opposition.
>
> The Pitch: "22-yards" long, where the main action happens.
>
> Batting: Two batters on the field at a time; they score runs by running between wickets or hitting boundaries.

Bowling: Bowler delivers 6 legal balls per over; aim is to dismiss batters and limit runs.

Scoring: Single (1), Four (boundary along ground), Six (boundary in the air), Extras (wides, no-balls, byes, leg-byes).

Outs: Bowled, caught, LBW, run out, stumped, hit wicket, and others.

Formats: Test (up to 5 days), ODI (50 overs/side), T20 (20 overs/side).

Spirit: Play fair, respect officials, enjoy the game.

CHAPTER FIVE: UNDERSTANDING THE GAME

Formats – Test, ODI, T20

Test Cricket

. **Length:** Up to 5 days long.

. **Ball & Clothing:** Uses a red ball and players wear traditional white kit.

. **How it works:** Each team bats twice (two innings each). The aim is to score more runs than the other team over the course of the match.

. **Style of play:** Considered the "purest" form of the game. Slower paced, with lots of strategy and patience needed.

ODI (One Day International)

. **Length:** One day, with 50 overs per side.

. **Ball & Clothing:** Uses a white ball and players wear coloured clothing.

. **How it works:** Each team bats once. An "over" is 6 balls bowled by the same bowler, so each team faces 300 balls maximum.

. **Style of play:** Balanced, not as long as Tests, but allows time for big scores and exciting chases.

T20 (Twenty20 Cricket)

. **Length:** Around 3 hours, with 20 overs per side.

. **Ball & Clothing:** Uses a white ball and players wear coloured clothing.

. **How it works:** Each team bats once, facing 120 balls maximum.

. **Style of play:** Fast, entertainment-focused, big hitting, quick scoring, music, and atmosphere in the stands.

40-Over Cricket *(Common in Grassroots Senior Cricket)*

. **Length:** Usually 5–6 hours in a single day, with 40 overs per side.

. **Ball & Clothing:** Can be red or white ball depending on the league, with either whites or coloured kit.

Why it's popular:

. Fits into one afternoon.

. Still allows time for tactical batting and bowling.

. Great balance between the traditional game and the excitement of shorter formats.

Where you'll see it:

Many Saturday and Sunday club leagues use this format for senior matches.

A typical scene for grass-roots players and fans during summer months.

CHAPTER SIX: INNINGS, OVERS, AND TURNS

Innings

. Think of an innings as a team's turn to bat.

. While one team bats and tries to score runs, the other team bowls and fields, trying to get them out.

. When the batting team's innings is over (all players are out or they've used up their overs), the teams swap roles.

Overs

. An over is six legal deliveries (balls) bowled by the same bowler.

. "Legal" means the ball is bowled fairly. If the bowler bowls a "no-ball" or "wide," it doesn't count towards the six and must be bowled again.

Switching Ends

After each over, the bowlers change ends.

. That means the next bowler delivers the ball from the opposite side of the pitch.

CHAPTER SEVEN: HOW TO SCORE RUNS

Running Runs

. **Single** – Run once to the other end = 1 run.

. **Two** – Run there and back again = 2 runs.

. **Three** – Run there, back, and there again = 3 runs.

. Both batters must run at the same time and get to the opposite end safely.

Boundaries

. **4 runs** – Ball touches or bounces before crossing the boundary rope.

. **6 runs** – Ball crosses the boundary rope without touching the ground (hit straight over)

Extras *(Runs given to the batting team without hitting the ball with the bat)*

. **Wide** – Bowled too far for the batter to reach.

. **No-ball** – Bowled illegally (e.g., overstepping the crease or dangerous delivery).

. **Bye** – Batter misses the ball, but it also misses the wicketkeeper, allowing a run.

. **Leg-bye** – Ball hits the batter's body (not the bat) and they run.

Running Safely

. To score a run, you must ground your bat (or part of your body) behind the popping crease at the other end.

. "Grounding your bat" means the bat is touching the ground inside the safe zone when you reach the end of your run.

. If you don't get your bat or body over the line before the stumps are hit, you can be run out.

CHAPTER EIGHT: GETTING OUT – ALL DISMISSALS

Main Ways

1. **Bowled** – The bowler delivers the ball, and it hits the stumps, knocking the bails off.

2. **Caught** – The batter hits the ball, and a fielder (including the bowler or wicketkeeper) catches it before it touches the ground.

3. **LBW (Leg Before Wicket)**[1] – If the ball would have hit the stumps but instead hits the batter's leg or pad in line with the stumps, they can be given out. The umpire also decides based on where the ball pitched, where it hit, and whether it was going to hit the stumps.

4. **Run Out** – A fielder hits the stumps with the ball before the batter has grounded their bat or body behind the popping crease while running between wickets.

5. **Stumped** – The wicketkeeper puts down the stumps while the batter is out of their crease and not trying to run, usually after stepping forward to play a ball.

6. **Hit Wicket** – The batter accidentally hits their own stumps with their bat, clothes, or body after the bowler has delivered the ball.

N.B. **"Where the ball was pitched"** In LBW this means the spot on the pitch where the ball bounced before it reached the batter.

In cricket, the umpire considers this because the laws say:

. For most LBW decisions, the ball must pitch either in line with the stumps or outside the line of the off stump.

. If the ball pitches outside the leg stump (the batter's leg side), you generally can't be out LBW even if it goes on to hit your pads in front of the stumps.

---

[1] At higher levels the LBW Law has a few extra technical details, but this is the version most players and coaches use day to day.

So, in simple terms:

. **Pitched = landed/bounced on the pitch** before hitting you.

. The umpire checks **which side of the stumps** the bounce was on, because that affects whether LBW is possible under the rules.

Less Common Ways of Getting Out

Alongside the common ways of getting out, such as bowled, caught, LBW, run out and stumped, a few dismissals are so uncommon that many players can go years without seeing one. They still appear in the Laws of Cricket, so it is useful to know they exist.

. **Timed Out** – The next batter takes too long (over two minutes in most formats) to be ready to face the next ball.

. **Hit the Ball Twice -** The striker is out if they deliberately hit the ball a second time after it has come off the bat. The only exception is if they are stopping the ball from rolling onto their stumps and they do it purely to protect their wicket.

. **Obstructing the Field-** A batter can be given out if they deliberately get in the way of a fielder who is trying to catch or collect the ball. The key word is deliberately.

. **Handling the Ball** - This used to be a separate dismissal for a batter deliberately touching the ball with their hand without the fielders' permission. The law was removed in 2017 and absorbed it into obstructing the field, since the actions are the same in practice. The behaviour is still illegal, but the old term is often used out of habit.

. **Retired Out** - If a batter leaves the field for a reason other than injury or illness, they can be marked as retired out. They can only return if the fielding captain agrees. This is normally seen only in friendly matches or unusual situations.

. **Double Hit on Purpose** - If a batter uses the bat to hit the ball twice to score runs, not to protect their stumps, they can be given out. This is a more technical version of hit the ball twice.

. **Obstructing a Catch** - If a batter prevents a fielder from taking a catch by word or action, they can be out. This sits under obstructing the field but is worth mentioning separately for clarity.

"You're Out!" – The Greatest Dismissal Tales in Cricket

Cricket is a game of moments: the cover-drive that pings through the field, the roar of a bowler when the stumps fly, the crowd's intake of breath as a ball soars toward the boundary. But perhaps no single moment carries more drama than the dismissal. In that instant, a batter's dreams can vanish, a bowler's plan can be vindicated, or an umpire can become the centre of attention.

And unlike runs or wickets tallied neatly in scorebooks, dismissals are personal. They stick in the memory funny, controversial, cruel, or character-revealing. Here is the tale of being "out," as told through some of the most famous stories in cricket history.

The Funny Outs

Inzamam-ul-Haq – Stumped by Himself
Few batters were as elegant as Inzamam, but few also managed such comic dismissals. In a 2006 ODI against England, he leaned back to cut, lost his balance, and crashed into his stumps. Out: hit wicket. The sight of the gentle giant sprawling on the turf left teammates and commentators struggling not to laugh.

Steve Harmison – The Nightwatchman Without a Night
Sent in as a Nightwatchman, (a lower-order batter sent in near the end of the day in a long match to protect better batters from having to bat in fading light) Harmison prepared for a gritty innings. He didn't even face a ball. Stranded out of his ground at the non-striker's end, he was run out before his vigil began. "I still think it was my best duck," he later joked.

Mark Richardson – The Slowest Run-Out in History
New Zealand opener Mark Richardson built a reputation as the slowest man alive between the wickets. In one infamous run-out, his partner gave up in despair as Richardson lumbered down the pitch. Teammates later teased him mercilessly: "You could have taken the bus!"

Andrew Flintoff – Out While Laughing

In a county game, Flintoff tried an agricultural slog that ballooned straight up. He chuckled as the ball descended, only to be caught comfortably at mid-on. He walked back to the pavilion still laughing, saying: "That was the worst shot in cricket history."

The Controversial Outs

Vinoo Mankad vs Bill Brown, 1947

Mankad ran out Australian opener Bill Brown at the non-striker's end before delivering the ball. Legal, yes. Sporting? Opinions divided. Seventy years later, "Mankading" still sparks pub debates and social media wars. Even Virat Kohli and Jos Buttler have been dragged into the controversy.

Jos Buttler vs R. Ashwin, IPL 2019

The debate reignited when Ashwin "Mankaded" Buttler in Jaipur. The Englishman stormed off, furious. Ashwin defended himself: "I was within my rights." The world split into two camps, law versus spirit.

Brian Luckhurst – Handled the Ball

Luckhurst was given out for the rarest of dismissals: picking up the ball with his bare hand to toss it to a fielder. No malice intended, but the laws were clear. It remains one of cricket's strangest "outs."

Kumar Sangakkara – Same Mistake, Bigger Stage

Even greats can slip. Sangakkara once patted the ball away with his hand to stop it hitting his stumps. Australians appealed; the umpire gave him out. Sangakkara later called it "the daftest thing I ever did on a cricket pitch."

The Heartbreak Outs

Sir Donald Bradman – Bowled for a Duck, The Oval 1948

The crowd rose to its feet, cheering the Don one last time. Four runs were all he needed for an average of 100. Eric Hollies bowled a googly first ball. Bradman played across, missed, and his stumps were shattered. Out for a duck. His final average: 99.94. The cruellest statistic in sport, and the most poetic.

Mithali Raj – Run Out by a Fingertip
In a World Cup semi-final, Raj was run out with her bat hovering millimetres above the ground. Replays sealed her fate. She later admitted: "That was the hardest moment, knowing I'd cost my team with something so small."

Ben Stokes – The Almost-Out in the Super Over
In the World Cup final, Stokes mistimed a lofted shot in the Super Over. For a moment, the ball hung in the air, and he thought England's dream was over. It fell short. England won. Later he wrote: "That one shot aged me ten years in two seconds."

Harmanpreet Kaur – Bowled by the Slowest Ball
During the 2023 Women's World Cup, a looping slower ball bowled India's captain. She walked off shaking her head, later admitting: "That ball could have been bowled by a 12-year-old, and I still missed it."

Why We Remember Being Out

Dismissals linger in memory because they're human moments.

. They make us laugh.

. They spark debate.

. They break hearts.

. They reveal character.

Centuries are glorious, but outs are relatable. Every cricketer, from playground to Test match, has known that feeling. It's the one thing that truly unites us all.

CHAPTER NINE: BOWLING STYLES AND DELIVERIES

Every cricket match starts the same way: a bowler with the ball in hand, running in to deliver the very first contest between bat and ball. Bowling isn't just about hurling the ball down the pitch; it's about skill, control, variation, and a touch of psychology. From fiery fast bowlers who intimidate with raw pace, to crafty spinners who deceive with guile and turn, bowlers are the driving force that shapes the rhythm of the game.

Fast Bowling

. **What it is:** Bowling the ball at high speed to rush the batter.

. **Pace:** The sheer speed of the ball. Top fast bowlers can reach 90mph (145kph), but even at club level, a good fast ball can feel quick.

. **Bounce:** How high the ball rises after hitting the pitch; a short-pitched ball can bounce up towards the batter's chest or head.

Spin Bowling

. **What it is:** Bowling the ball more slowly but with a lot of spin so it turns after bouncing.

. **Off-break:** Spins from the batter's off-side **towards** their leg-side (for a right-handed batter, from right to left).

. **Leg-break:** Spins from the batter's leg-side **towards** their off-side (for a right-handed batter, from left to right).

Bowling Variations *(Used by both fast and spin bowlers)*

. **Yorker:** Bowled so it lands right at the batter's feet, making it hard to hit.

. **Bouncer:** Short-pitched ball that bounces high, aiming to surprise or intimidate.

. **Slower Ball:** Looks like a normal delivery but bowled at a lower speed to trick the batter into playing too early.

. **Cutter:** A fast ball with a small amount of spin. It grips the pitch and changes direction slightly after bouncing.

Arm and release: When you bowl, your bowling arm should stay straight at the elbow (no bending like a throw, A slight natural flex is allowed, but not a visible bend-and-straighten). Let go of the ball *before* your front foot touches or lands beyond the crease (the line on the pitch).

Where to aim: Try to land the ball on the pitch so it bounces close to where the batter's front foot would be when they play a shot, not too close to them, but not too far away either. This is called a "good length."

Run-up: Find a short, comfortable starting position to run in from. Do the same steps each time so your run-up feels natural and consistent.

What to focus on first: Don't worry about speed yet. Work on bowling the ball in the same good spot again and again. Accuracy is the key when starting out.

Bowling – Imagine You're Skimming a Stone

Straight arm:
Think of bowling like swinging your arm to skim a stone over water; your arm stays straight as it comes over. In cricket, you can't bend the elbow like a baseball throw.

When to let go:
Release the ball just before your front foot reaches the "no-ball line" (the crease) on the pitch. If you let go after your foot crosses the line, it's a no-ball.

Where to aim:
Picture a welcome mat in front of the batter. You want the ball to bounce on that mat, far enough away so they can't easily hit it, but close enough to make them think. That's the "good length."

Run-up:
Like starting a dance move or a routine in gymnastics, you want the same number of steps every time, so your body gets used to the rhythm.

Priority:
Before worrying about bowling fast, practise hitting your "welcome mat" target again and again. Accuracy beats power for beginners.

Different Types of Bowling and Deliveries

Bowling in cricket comes in many styles and variations. Bowlers use different grips, speeds, and wrist actions to produce deliveries that challenge the batter in different ways. Here's a guide to the main types of bowling and some common deliveries you'll encounter:

. **Carrom Ball:** Flicked from the fingers to create unpredictable spin.

- **Doosra:** An off-spinner's variation that turns the opposite way.

- **Topspinner:** A spin ball that drops quicker and bounces higher than expected.

- **Flipper:** A leg-spin delivery that skids low after pitching.

- **Googly:** A leg-spinner's ball that spins the opposite way, surprising the batter.

- **Leg-Spin:** Turns from leg to off-side for a right-hander. Includes variations like the googly and flipper.

- **Off-Spin:** Turns from off to leg-side for a right-hander. Includes variations like the arm ball.

- **Spin Bowling:** Delivered at a slower pace with wrist or finger action to turn the ball. Includes off-spin and leg-spin.

- **Swing Bowling:** Uses the shiny and rough sides of the ball to make it curve in the air. Outswing moves away from the batter; inswing moves in.

- **Seam Bowling:** Focuses on landing the ball on the seam to create movement off the pitch.

- **Fast Bowling:** Relies on speed and bounce to trouble the batter. Variations include outswing, inswing, Yorkers, and bouncers.

Masters of the Ball: Famous Bowlers and Their Styles

Cricket is often called a batter's game, but it is the bowlers who breathe life into it. They are the artists, the crafters, and sometimes the magicians, conjuring swing, spin, and sheer terror from 22 yards away. Throughout history, men and women have defined their eras with the ball, their names forever tied to the style they perfected.

Fast Bowlers (Pace and Fire)

- **Fred Trueman (England)** – "Fiery Fred," the first to 300 Test wickets, aggressive and fiercely Yorkshire.

. **Dennis Lillee (Australia)** – 1970s icon, moustache bristling, charging in with raw pace and swagger.

. **Jeff Thomson (Australia)** – Slinging action, extreme pace, and terror in tandem with Lillee.

. **Malcolm Marshall (West Indies)** – Short in stature but lethal, perhaps the most complete fast bowler ever.

. **Curtly Ambrose (West Indies)** – Towering presence, miserly in runs, devastating with bounce.

. **Waqar Younis (Pakistan)** – Toe-crushing Yorkers, Akram's lethal partner.

. **Dale Steyn (South Africa)** – Express pace, wicked outswing, and modern menace.

. **Cathryn Fitzpatrick (Australia)** – The fastest of her era in the women's game, spearheading two World Cups with sheer pace.

. **Jhulan Goswami (India)** – The "Chakdaha Express," highest women's ODI wicket-taker, famed for bounce and swing.

. **Katherine Sciver-Brunt (England)** – Fiery and passionate, England's leader with the ball for almost two decades.

. **Shabnim Ismail (South Africa)** – Modern quick, regularly exceeding 120 km/h, rattling top orders.

. **Ellyse Perry (Australia)** – All-round legend, with match-winning fast-medium spells including 7 for 22 in the 2019 Ashes.

Swing Bowlers

. **James Anderson (England)** – Master of the swinging Duke's ball, England's record wicket-taker.

. **Stuart Broad (England)** – Tall, rhythmic, destructive in bursts (notably 8 for 15 vs Australia, 2015).

. **Richard Hadlee (New Zealand)** – Kiwi craftsman, carrying his nation's attack.

. **Anya Shrubsole (England)** – Hero of the 2017 Women's World Cup Final, 6 for 46 at Lord's.

. **Megan Schutt (Australia)** – Deadly inswingers and clever variations in white-ball cricket.

. **Marizanne Kapp (South Africa)** – World-class seam bowling all-rounder, partnership-breaker, and match-winner.

Spin Wizards (The Magicians)

Leg-Spin:

. **Shane Warne (Australia)** – Revolutionised leg-spin, famous for the "Ball of the Century."

. **Abdul Qadir (Pakistan)** – The magician of the 1980s, mentor to many.

. **Anil Kumble (India)** – Relentless accuracy and bounce, 619 Test wickets.

. **Poonam Yadav (India)** – Loopy leg-breaks that stunned Australia in the 2020 T20 World Cup.

. **Alana King (Australia)** – Modern star, Commonwealth Games hat-trick hero.

Off-Spin:

. **Muttiah Muralitharan (Sri Lanka)** – Record-holder with 800 Test wickets, master of the doosra.

. **Jim Laker (England)** – 19 wickets in a single Test (1956).

. **Neetu David (India)** – Best Test figures in women's cricket: 8 for 53.

. **Lisa Sthalekar (Australia)** – Off-spinning all-rounder, match-winner in tight games.

Left-Arm Spin:

. **Bishan Singh Bedi (India)** – Guile and artistry, part of India's great spin quartet.

. **Daniel Vettori (New Zealand)** – Accurate, economical, and a leader with the ball.

. **Sophie Ecclestone (England)** – World No. 1 T20I bowler, tall, calm, and devastating.

. **Enid Bakewell (England, 1960s–70s)** – Combined spin with batting brilliance, one of the first true female all-rounders.

All-Round Impact

. **Kapil Dev (India)** – bowling all-rounder, led India to the 1983 World Cup.

. **Imran Khan (Pakistan)** – Inspirational captain, fast bowler, and 1992 World Cup winner.

. **Sir Ian Botham (England)** – Outswing spells and match-turning charisma.

. **Heather Knight (England)** – Skipper and primarily a batter, but handy occasional off-spin has produced surprise breakthroughs.

Why They Matter

From Lillee's fire to Fitzpatrick's speed, from Warne's guile to Ecclestone's calm mastery, the story of cricket is as much about bowlers as batters. Men and women alike have bent games to their will with spells that redefined possibility.

Batters may score the runs, but bowlers write the drama. They deliver the unplayable ball, the devastating spell, the miracle at Lord's or the yorker under lights. And in those moments, whether it's Wasim Akram reversing a ball late at pace, or Anya Shrubsole swinging England to a World Cup, cricket reminds us that the ball, not just the bat, shapes its greatest legends.

CHAPTER TEN: BATTING STROKES – FROM DEFENCE TO REVERSE SWEEP

Forward Defence

. Step forward towards the ball with your front foot.

. Use your bat like a shield to block the ball safely onto the ground.

. Used against good-length balls that could hit the stumps.

Back Foot Defence

. Step back towards the stumps, giving yourself more time.

. Block the ball down if it bounces higher or is bowled short.

. Good for defending against fast, short deliveries.

Straight Drive

. Step forward and hit the ball straight down the ground past the bowler.

- Played with a vertical bat and full follow-through.

- A safe, powerful scoring shot for straight deliveries.

Cut Shot

- Played to a short, wide ball outside the off stump.

- Use a horizontal bat to hit the ball square or behind square on the off-side.

Pull Shot

- Played to a short ball around chest height.

- Rotate your body and pull the ball to the leg-side, usually between mid-wicket and square leg.

Sweep Shot

- Kneel on one leg and swing the bat in a horizontal arc.

- Aimed to hit balls pitched on or outside leg stump, rolling along the ground to the leg-side.

Reverse Sweep *(Advanced)*

- Like a normal sweep, but you swap the bat's direction mid-shot.

- Hit the ball into the off-side by reversing your grip and stance slightly.

Key Batting Tips for All Shots

- **Head Still:** Keeps your balance and helps judge the ball's line and length.

- **Watch the Ball:** From the bowler's hand all the way until it hits your bat.

Grip (holding the bat):
Imagine holding a broom to sweep the floor. Your hands are close together on the handle. The *top* hand (nearest the broom head/bat blade) is the driver; it steers where the bat goes. The *bottom* hand is the "passenger" it just helps and follows along.

Stance (how you stand):
Pretend you're waiting for someone to throw you a ball in the garden. Turn sideways so your shoulder is facing them, not your chest. Your feet should be as far apart as your shoulders, knees slightly bent, like you're ready to spring into action.

First shots (what to try first):
Don't try to smash it! First, learn how to stop the ball safely (blocking/defence). Then practise pushing it gently back past the bowler (straight drive), a bit like rolling a football back to them. Once you can hit it in the middle of the bat regularly, *then* you can start adding power.

How to Hit a Cricket Ball: The Batter's Dictionary of Shots

One of cricket's great joys is that no two batters play quite the same way. Some glide the ball like an artist painting brushstrokes. Others treat the ball as if it owes them money and must be dispatched into the car park. Over the centuries, a whole language of shots has developed some elegant, some ugly, some frankly ridiculous.

Here's your guide to the strokes that make up batting's rich vocabulary:

Classic Cricket Shots

These are the textbook strokes every batter learns:

- **Forward Defence** – the classic, bat angled forward to block. The pose every coach loves: bat angled, elbow high, head over the ball. Less about scoring runs, more about looking like you know what you're doing.

. **Back Foot Defence** – same idea but played from the back foot.

. **Straight Drive** – hit straight down the ground past the bowler. The most beautiful shot in cricket. Played down the ground, often with commentators sighing: *"Oh, that's a proper cricket shot."*

. **Cover Drive** – driven through the covers (between extra cover and mid-off). Elegant flourish through extra cover. The hallmark of batters who like their name written in calligraphy.

. **Off Drive** – between cover and mid-off.

. **On Drive** – between mid-on and straight down the ground. Both Off and On Driving are on either side of the bowler. Stylish when executed, agricultural when not.

. **Square Drive** – hit square through the off-side. Played square on the off-side, usually off the back foot. Great for showing off quick hands.

. **Pull Shot** – back-foot shot to a short ball, pulled to mid-wicket.

. **Hook Shot** – similar to the pull but played to a bouncer, often above head height. Both Pull & Hook are taking on the short ball with aggression. The pull is waist-high; the hook is for when the bowler is trying to rearrange your teeth.

. **Cut Shot** – square of the wicket on the off-side, usually from a short, wide ball.

. **Leg Glance** – turned fine on the leg side.

. **Flick** – more forceful version of the leg glance. Leg Glance and Flick are both a delicate nudge off the pads, often enough to earn you "four runs, thank you very much."

Aggressive / Power Shots

. **Lofted Drive** – an aerial shot to clear the infield. Like a cover drive but airborne, aimed over the infield. Risky, but glorious.

. **Slog** – an unorthodox, hard hit usually to the leg-side. Not in the textbook. A heave-ho, usually cow-corner-bound. Tailenders' favourite.

. **Slog Sweep** – a cross-batted slog against a spinner. Cross between a sweep and a baseball swing. Popular in T20s.

. **Sweep** – kneeling shot played against spin, sweeping the ball on the leg side. Kneel, sweep across the line. The traditional spinner's nightmare.

. **Reverse Sweep** – switching grip/stance and sweeping to the off-side. Same idea but flipped to the off-side. Causes gasps when it works, groans when it doesn't.

. **Ramp / Scoop** – using the pace of the bowler to flick the ball over the wicketkeeper. Using the bowler's pace to deflect the ball over the keeper's head. A crowd-pleaser and a heart-stopper for the bowler.

. **Switch Hit** – swapping from right-handed to left-handed mid-delivery (famously used by Kevin Pietersen). Mid-delivery, you flip from right-hander to left-hander. Kevin Pietersen made it famous; many club cricketers make it disastrous.

. **Helicopter Shot** – MS Dhoni's signature shot, whipping the bat through with wrists to generate power. Need wrists of steel to whip the ball into orbit. Don't try this at your village nets.

. **Uppercut** – deliberately cutting a short ball over the slips or gully.

More Informal / Slang Terms

. **Ramp Shot / Dilscoop** – named after Tilakaratne Dilshan, the pioneer of scooping balls over his head. Using the bowler's pace to deflect the ball over the keeper's head. A crowd-pleaser and a heart-stopper for the bowler.

. **Reverse Ramp** – scoop but played with reversed hands.

. **Inside-out Shot** – stepping away to hit a ball over the off-side.

The "What Was That?" Shots

. **Hoick** – A wild, ungainly swipe to the leg side. Ugly but effective, the cricketing equivalent of ordering beans on toast at a five-star restaurant.

. **Dab** – A delicate prod guiding the ball to third man. Often used in T20s when sixes aren't strictly necessary.

. **Inside-Out Shot** – Stepping away and lofting the ball over extra cover. Risky, but makes you look like a genius when it works.

. **Fine Inside Edge (formerly known as French Cut / Chinese Cut**)– A thick inside edge that misses your stumps by a whisker and runs down to fine leg. Equal parts comedy and relief.

. **Agricultural Shot** – A wild mow across the line, favoured by farmers and No. 11s. Sometimes clears cow corner, sometimes just clears your dignity.

. **Cow Shot** – A slog aimed at deep mid-wicket, named after the pasture beyond the boundary. Classic Sunday-league stroke.

. **Periscope** – Bouncer flies past, bat raised vertically like a submarine periscope. Usually accidental, always hilarious.

Regional/Modern Twists

. **Paddle Sweep** – popular in subcontinental cricket.

. **Periscope** – letting a bouncer hit the bat raised vertically, often accidental!

. **Reverse Ramp** – Jos Buttler favourite.

. **Bazball Hits** – England's current style has normalised constant reverse sweeps and ramps in Test cricket.

The Batter's Dictionary of Shots (with Legends)

Batting in cricket isn't just about survival; it's about expression. Over the centuries, shots have taken on names, quirks, and, in some cases, legendary players who perfected them. Here's your **A–Z of strokes,** from the elegant to the eccentric and the players who made them famous.

Cricket's Great Shots: Men & Women Who Perfected Them.

The Classics:

. **Forward Defence** – The very image of Test cricket.

. *Men:* Rahul Dravid, nicknamed *"The Wall"*, built entire careers on it.

. *Women:* Mithali Raj, India's greatest Test run-scorer, played the defensive shot with unshakeable patience.

. **Straight Drive** – Poetry in motion.

. *Men:* Sachin Tendulkar's straight drive was so pure it often got a standing ovation.

. *Women:* Smriti Mandhana has been hailed as Tendulkar's heir in elegance, her straight drive just as graceful.

. **Cover Drive** – The most elegant shot in cricket.

. *Men:* Virat Kohli and Ian Bell both made fans swoon with theirs.

. *Women:* Meg Lanning, Australia's captain, has one of the crispest cover drives in the women's game.

. **On Drive / Off Drive** – Graceful but harder to master.

. *Men:* VVS Laxman, the on-drive king, timing it with liquid wrists.

. *Women:* Claire Taylor (England) played these with textbook perfection in her peak 2009 World Cup.

. **Square Cut** – A scorcher through point.

. *Men:* Sir Jack Hobbs and Brian Lara carved these with devastating ease.

. *Women:* Charlotte Edwards, England's long-time skipper, was a square-cut machine.

. **Pull Shot** – Controlled aggression.

. *Men:* Ricky Ponting turned the pull into an art, often smacking bowlers into the stands.

. *Women:* Harmanpreet Kaur's famous 171* vs Australia in the 2017 World Cup featured blistering pull shots.

. **Hook Shot** – The bravest shot against fast bowling.

. *Men:* Viv Richards and Gordon Greenidge made the hook their weapon of choice.

. *Women:* Shafali Verma, India's fearless opener, has already made the hook her trademark at just 19.

. **Leg Glance / Flick** – Wristy and delicate.

. *Men:* Mohammad Azharuddin and KL Rahul.

. *Women:* Suzie Bates (New Zealand) uses the flick to accumulate runs with effortless timing.

The Power Shots (Crowd-Pleasers)

. **Sweep** – The spinner's nightmare.

. *Men:* Graham Gooch and Matthew Hayden swept spinners into submission.

. *Women:* Tammy Beaumont (England) and Chamari Athapaththu (Sri Lanka) dominate with the sweep.

. **Reverse Sweep** – Once outrageous, now routine.

. *Men:* Andy Flower popularised it; Jos Buttler perfected it.

. *Women:* Danni Wyatt (England) and Lizelle Lee (South Africa) are fearless reverse sweepers.

. **Slog** – Power over style.

. *Men:* Shahid Afridi turned it into a match-winning weapon.

. *Women:* Deandra Dottin (West Indies) smashed the fastest-ever women's T20 century with slogging power.

. **Slog Sweep** – Controlled chaos.

. *Men:* Kevin Pietersen and Eoin Morgan.

. *Women:* Sophie Devine (New Zealand) clears ropes with the slog sweep like few others.

. **Lofted Drive** – Elegance with altitude.

. *Men:* Chris Gayle, the *"Universe Boss".*

. *Women:* Alyssa Healy (Australia) has thrilled crowds lofting drives in World Cup finals.

. **Helicopter Shot** – Purely MS Dhoni.

. *Men:* MS Dhoni redefined finishing.

. *Women:* Jemimah Rodrigues (India) has played helicopter-style whips in T20s.

. **Ramp / Scoop** – Audacious invention.

. *Men:* Dilshan's *"Dilscoop",* expanded by AB de Villiers.

. *Women:* Nat Sciver-Brunt's scoop is so famous it's nicknamed the *"Natmeg."*

. **Switch-Hit** – High-risk artistry.

. *Men:* Kevin Pietersen stunned the world by hitting Murali this way.

. *Women:* Sophie Devine has pulled off switch-hits in international T20s.

Modern Innovations

. **Dil-scoop** – Dilshan's party trick.

. *Men:* Tillakaratne Dilshan.

. *Women:* Nat Sciver-Brunt often scoops over fine leg in T20s.

. **Reverse Ramp** – Bold, brave.

. *Men:* Jos Buttler.

. *Women:* Danni Wyatt uses it to stun bowlers in the powerplay.

. **Bazball Specials** – Redefining Test batting.

. *Men:* Ben Stokes, Jonny Bairstow, playing T20 shots on Day One.

. *Women:* England's Sophia Dunkley and Alice Capsey bring fearless *Bazball* spirit to the women's game.

A quick recap of where the most famous cricket shots go on the field.

. **Straight Drive** = down the ground.

. **Cover Drive** = through the covers.

. **Square Cut / Uppercut** = off-side, square or behind.

. **Pull / Hook / Cow Corner** = leg-side boundary.

. **Sweep / Slog Sweep / Leg Glance** = classic leg-side shots.

. **Reverse Sweep** = the cheeky one into the off-side.

From Dravid's wall-like defence to Mandhana's sublime cover drives, from Ponting's pull to Kaur's fearless slog sweeps, every shot has its masters and mistresses. Men may have defined many strokes first, but women have embraced, perfected, and in some cases reinvented them for the modern game. Cricket's shot-making is now a truly shared heritage, across genders and across generations.

CHAPTER ELEVEN: FIELDING EXPLAINED

Fielding is where cricket comes alive between the bat and the ball. While batting and bowling often steal the headlines, sharp fielding can turn matches just as quickly. A brilliant catch, a lightning-fast run-out, or simply cutting off boundaries with energy and awareness can shift momentum in an instant. Good fielding is about anticipation, teamwork, and commitment, less glamorous but equally vital art that keeps the game ticking and wins the tightest contests.

Key Fielding Positions in Cricket

Close to the Batter – Slip Fielders

. **Slips** – Stand just behind the batter on the off-side (same side as the bat face).

. Purpose: Catch balls that edge off the bat and fly behind.

. Usually, a line of 1 to 4 fielders next to the wicketkeeper.

Off-Side Positions

. **Gully** – Between slips and point, ready for edged balls that don't carry to slips.

. **Point** – Square (side-on) to the batter on the off-side, ready for cuts and square drives.

. **Cover** – In front of point but further toward the bowler, stopping drives through the off-side.

. **Mid-off** – Straight, closer to the bowler on the off-side, stopping balls hit straight down the ground.

Leg-Side Positions *(Same side as the batter's legs)*

. **Mid-on** – Same as mid-off but on the leg-side of the pitch.

. **Square Leg** – Square (side-on) to the batter on the leg-side, waiting for pulls and hooks.

. **Fine Leg** – Behind the batter on the leg-side, near the boundary, stopping glances and deflections.

Boundary Off-Side

. **Third Man** – Behind the batter on the off-side near the boundary, stopping edged balls that pass slips and gully.

Diagram of fielding positions adapted from miljoshi & Stevage, *Cricket fielding positions2.svg*, licensed under CC BY-SA 3.0 / GFDL

Quick Tip for Beginners:

. *Off-side* = the side of a cricket field the batter's body faces when batting. For example, the right-hand-side of the field for a right-handed batter.

. *Leg-side* = the side of the batter's legs and back.

. Positions are named the same whether you're playing professional or grassroots cricket.

Catching:
When catching the ball, keep your eyes level and watch it all the way into your hands. Let your hands move back slightly as the ball arrives. This is called having *soft hands, and* it stops the ball from bouncing out.

Ground fielding:
When stopping the ball on the ground, use the *long barrier* for safety: kneel or put one leg behind your hands so if the ball slips past, your body stops it. Pick the ball up and throw it in using a quick, steady action don't rush so much that you lose balance.

Backing up (what it means):

When batting: If you're the non-striker (not hitting the ball), walk or jog a few steps down the pitch as your partner plays the shot. If they run, you're already moving; if they don't, you can quickly get back.

. *When fielding*: Stand in a position behind the fielder who is stopping or throwing the ball. If the ball slips past them or their throw misses its target, you're there to collect it before it goes too far.

In short, backing up means being ready to help your teammate if the ball gets past them, so the team doesn't lose precious runs or waste time.

The Greatest Fielding Stories of All Time

Cricket was not always a fielder's game. For decades, batters took centre stage, bowlers set the scene, and fielders were… well, largely extras. But over time, fielders became the actors who stole the show, the ones who redefined possibility, snatched victory from defeat, and left jaws on the ground. Here are the tales of those who turned fielding into art.

1. The Legend of Eknath Solkar (1970s)

Before Jonty Rhodes, there was Eknath Solkar, India's close-in catching genius. Fielding at short leg, helmet-less, inches from the bat, Solkar pouched 53 catches in just 27 Tests, still a record for a non-wicketkeeper with so few matches. His bravery gave India's spinners the confidence to attack relentlessly. Solkar once said: *"I only smell the ball, I don't see it."*

2. Kapil Dev's World Cup Miracle (1983)

Lord's, World Cup Final. Viv Richards launched a skied pull that looked destined for the stands. Kapil Dev ran backwards from mid-wicket, never taking his eyes off the ball, and clung on safely. That single moment flipped the match, India won their first World Cup, and a legend was sealed.

3. Paul Collingwood's Aerobatics (2005)

Against Australia at Bristol, Collingwood launched himself one-handed to dismiss Matthew Hayden. It wasn't just a catch; it was belief. For once, England could match Australia on the field. That summer ended with the Ashes back in English hands.

4. Sarah Taylor's Lightning Gloves (2009)

Women's Ashes, against Australia. A faint edge flew behind the stumps, and standing up to the bowler, Sarah Taylor reacted in a blink, snaffling it cleanly. It redefined wicketkeeping standards worldwide.

5. Suzie Bates' Superman Catch (2018)

Against South Africa, New Zealand's Suzie Bates launched herself full-stretch at point, plucking the ball inches from the turf. Even the batter applauded. Bates, usually celebrated for her batting, proved she was just as capable of match-turning brilliance in the field.

6. Ben Stokes' Catch of the Century (2019)

World Cup opener at The Oval. Andile Phehlukwayo miscued a cut, Stokes sprinted, leapt, twisted mid-air, and clung on one-handed, airborne and horizontal. "No way!" gasped the commentators. Social media exploded. That moment lit the fuse on England's World Cup win.

7. Ellyse Perry's Boundary Miracle (2019)

Ashes Test at Taunton. Perry backpedalled at the rope, juggling the ball once, twice, before clutching it inches from the advertising boards. Calm, athletic, and star quality in one moment. It symbolised the rise of women's cricket as a spectacle equal to the men's game.

Why Fielding Stories Matter

Cricket's magic doesn't only come from centuries or five-wicket hauls. Sometimes it's a single leap, a desperate dive, or the sound of stumps flying that fans remember for a lifetime.

- Fielding creates instant drama. The gasp, the silence, the roar.

- It embodies team spirit. Bodies on the line for the side.

- It inspires the next generation. Every child diving on a school field is chasing their own Jonty, Perry, or Stokes moment.

As the saying goes: *"Catches win matches."* But the very best fielding stories do something bigger; they win hearts, rewrite what's possible, and remind us that cricket, at its core, is about joy, daring, and the impossible made real.

CHAPTER TWELVE. UMPIRES, SIGNALS, AND DECISIONS.

Cricket would descend into chaos without umpires. They are the guardians of the Laws, the calm figures in white (or now sometimes neon!) who control the flow of the game. From raising a finger to signal a batter's dismissal to spreading their arms wide for a six, their signals are a language of cricket in themselves. Understanding these decisions not only helps you follow the action but also reveals just how much authority and pressure rests on the umpire's shoulders.

Four runs – Arms waved horizontally.

Six runs – Both arms raised above head.

Out – Finger pointed up.

Wide – Both arms stretched out horizontally.

No-ball – One arm stretched out horizontally.

Byes – One hand raised above head, palm open.

Leg-byes – One leg tapped with the hand.

The Invisible Giants

For every six smashed into the stands or wicket cartwheeling down the pitch, there's a quieter heartbeat keeping the game alive: the umpire. Their role is paradoxical, essential, but ideally unnoticed. An umpire's perfect day is one where nobody remembers them. And yet, cricket has given us umpires whose quirks, courage, and controversies made them unforgettable.

This is their story: the guardians of the game, the characters who made crowds laugh, the figures who kept their calm in chaos, and the pioneers who broke barriers.

In the Beginning

In cricket's earliest days, umpires were often players from the opposing side, hardly the recipe for neutrality. Matches in the 18th and 19th centuries saw arguments, brawls, and accusations of bias. One famous 19th-century complaint read: *"We should have won had the umpire remembered his spectacles."*

By the 20th century, neutral umpires became the norm, and the role slowly professionalised. White coats became iconic. The finger raised heavenward became one of sport's most recognisable gestures.

The Golden Age of Characters

Dickie Bird[2] – Yorkshire Wit and World Fame

No umpire has ever become more of a celebrity than Harold "Dickie" Bird. He stood in three World Cup finals, countless Tests, and yet his greatest gift was making the crowd laugh.

At Old Trafford, a pigeon refused to move from square leg. Bird halted play. "I can't have a pigeon killed on my watch," he said. Ian Botham barked back: *"Bird, the pigeon's safer than I am if you don't get on with it."*

---

[2] This book was completed shortly before the passing of Harold Dennis "Dickie" Bird OBE (1933–2025), the beloved Yorkshire umpire whose contribution to cricket remains unmatched.

His friendship with players was legendary. Yet he was fearless: he gave Geoffrey Boycott, his Yorkshire mate, out LBW at Headingley. Boycott never forgave him. "He was plumb," Bird said later. "But Geoffrey wouldn't admit it if the ball hit middle stump."

David Shepherd – The Hop at Nelson

If Bird was the comedian, David Shepherd was the kindly uncle. The round-faced Englishman umpired over 170 internationals, but what made him iconic was his superstition.

Whenever the score reached 111, "Nelson" Shepherd lifted one leg and hopped, convinced the number brought bad luck. Soon, entire stadiums joined in. The sight of 20,000 people bouncing in unison made Shepherd grin.

Even players joined the fun. Shane Warne once deliberately slowed play on 111 to keep Shepherd hopping longer. Shepherd wagged a finger at him: *"You're cruel, Shane."*

Steve Bucknor – The Calm in the Storm

Jamaica's Steve Bucknor was known as "Slow Death." His LBW decisions came after the longest pauses in cricket history. Batters often half-walked, unsure if they were dismissed.

Brian Lara quipped: *"With Bucknor, you had time for a sandwich before the finger went up."*

But Bucknor's calmness was his strength. At Eden Gardens in 2001, when crowd riots broke out during India's Test against Australia, Bucknor kept the players calm and helped avoid chaos. He stood in five World Cup finals, more than any umpire before or since.

The Women Who Changed the Game

Kathy Cross – The Pioneer

In 2016, New Zealand's Kathy Cross walked out to umpire at the Women's T20 World Cup. She was the first woman ever to stand in an ICC global event. She admitted to nerves but called it *"just cricket, once the first ball was bowled."*

Cross opened the door for others, proving gender was no barrier to sharp eyes and steady judgment.

Claire Polosak – Breaking the ODI Barrier

In 2019, Claire Polosak became the first woman to umpire a men's ODI. The occasion was celebrated worldwide.

She remembered a junior once yelling: *"I don't have to listen to you, you're a woman!"* Her reply was pure authority: *"You're out twice, once in cricket, once in manners."*

Later, she gave Chris Gayle LBW in a Caribbean Premier League match. Gayle winked and said: "First woman to give me out. I'll remember you." Polosak shot back: "Good. Don't do it again."

Sue Redfern – Trusted and Respected

England's Sue Redfern, now a familiar face in The Hundred, is admired by players. Heather Knight once said: *"Sue knows my game too well, I can't argue with her calls."*

Redfern reflects: *"It's a privilege to stand so close to the best in the world, and sometimes, it's a privilege to tell them they're out."*

Famous Umpire Stories About Players

. **Kapil Dev and David Shepherd**: After a marginal LBW appeal, Kapil teased: *"If I were bowling, you'd have given it."* Shepherd replied: *"If you bowled straighter, maybe."*

. **Aleem Dar and Virat Kohli**: After one explosive argument, Dar calmed him: *"Virat, you're too good to lose your head. Save it for the runs."* Kohli later said he remembered those words.

. **Billy Bowden and Andrew Flintoff**: Bowden's crooked finger became world famous. Flintoff mimicked him mid-match. Bowden grinned back: *"Nice try, Fred, but the copyright's mine."*

The DRS Era

With technology came new pressure. "You used to argue with batsmen," said Aleem Dar. "Now you wait for Hawk-Eye to argue with you."

Billy Bowden added: *"In my day, you were right or wrong. Now you're right, wrong, or 'Umpire's Call.'"*

The Hardest Job in Cricket

Umpires face battles players rarely see:

. **Heat:** Shepherd once lost half a stone umpiring in Chennai's 40°C furnace.

. **Crowds:** Bucknor endured death threats in India after a wrong call against Tendulkar.

. **Pressure:** In World Cup finals, every decision can echo forever.

Dickie Bird summed it up: *"You walk out with 22 players, and 21 are against you."*

Why Umpires Matter

For all the laughter and controversy, umpires are guardians of cricket's spirit.

David Shepherd said: *"We'll make mistakes, but the job is fairness. If both teams trust you, that's victory."*

And Dickie Bird, reflecting on his life in cricket, said: *"I loved every ball, every laugh, every player who cursed me. I'd do it all again tomorrow."*

Quiet Heroes

Cricket will always be about runs and wickets. But sometimes, the game is defined by the people who don't bat, don't bowl, and don't field.

The umpire's finger raised, Shepherd's hop, Bucknor's long pause, Polosak's history-making walk, these are as much a part of cricket's soul as any six or hat-trick.

As every player knows: the bowler may roar, the batter may plead, the crowd may scream, but in the end, all eyes turn to the umpire.

CHAPTER THIRTEEN: STAYING SAFE – PROTECTIVE GEAR AND INJURY PREVENTION

Cricket may be seen from afar as a sedate game, but a hard leather ball travelling at over 90 miles per hour is anything but sedate. That's why modern players step onto the field equipped with an array of protective gear, from helmets and pads to gloves and guards, designed to keep them safe. Whether you're a professional facing a world-class fast bowler or a beginner in the nets, understanding how to protect yourself is just as important as learning how to bat or bowl.

Helmet

. **What it does:** Protects your head, face, and jaw from being hit by the hard cricket ball, which can travel very fast.

. **When to wear it:**

. Always when batting against a hard ball.

. Always when fielding close to the batter (especially at silly point, short leg, or short cover).

. **Why it's important:** A cricket ball is solid leather and can cause serious injury if it hits your head. Helmets absorb and spread the impact to keep you safe.

Wicketkeeper Gear

. **Pads:** Special wicketkeeping pads are lighter and shaped to make crouching and moving easier.

. **Gloves:** Large, padded gloves with webbing between the thumb and fingers to catch balls safely.

. **Helmet or face guard:** Worn when standing close to the stumps to protect against fast deliveries.

. **Box (abdomen guard):** Protects the groin area from injury.

What You Cannot Wear When Fielding (except wicketkeeper)

. **Gloves:** Fielders (other than the wicketkeeper) are not allowed to wear catching gloves. You must use bare hands to stop or catch the ball; even padded gloves are not allowed.

. **Extra protective padding:** You can wear shin guards or a box if fielding close to the batter, but not anything that gives you an unfair advantage catching the ball.

Other Safety Tips

. **Warm up shoulders and hips:** Prevents muscle strains and injuries, especially if you're bowling or throwing a lot.

- **Hydration:** Drink water regularly, even if you don't feel thirsty.

- **Sunscreen:** Protects skin from sunburn during long matches.

- **Breaks:** Rest when possible, to avoid heat exhaustion and maintain focus.

Safety equipment is essential to the game, but sometimes accidents do happen. Here are some of the most famous injuries in cricket history, across men's and women's cricket, where the story of the injury became part of the sport's folklore. Some are horrific, some inspirational, and some almost unbelievable.

Bruised, Broken, but Unbowed – The Famous Injuries That Shaped Cricket

Cricket may be played in whites and often described as "a gentleman's game," but beneath the polite applause and rolling greens lies a sport that has tested the bodies, and sometimes the lives, of its players. Injuries have changed careers, altered destinies, and even rewritten the rules of safety. Some were tragic, some heroic, and others simply bizarre, but all left a mark on the story of cricket.

When the Game Turned Dangerous

In 1962, Indian captain Nari Contractor faced Charlie Griffith in Barbados. A short-pitched delivery smashed into his skull, fracturing it so badly he needed emergency surgery. Contractor spent days in a coma and never played Test cricket again. His injury was a wake-up call, long before helmets were widely used.

More than 50 years later, cricket was rocked again. In November 2014, Australian batter Phil Hughes was struck on the neck by a bouncer in a domestic match. He collapsed instantly and passed away two days later. He was just 25. Hughes' death shook the cricketing world to its core and forced urgent changes to helmet design and safety standards. It was the darkest reminder that cricket, for all its elegance, can be brutally unforgiving.

Acts of Courage

Some injuries didn't end careers; instead, they forged legends. In 2002, Anil Kumble had his jaw broken by a bouncer in Antigua. Most players would have flown home immediately. Kumble instead wrapped his face in bandages, came out to bowl, and dismissed Brian Lara. "I've broken my jaw, but I'm not letting the team down," he said. That image of Kumble bowling through pain became an instant symbol of grit.

Almost 20 years earlier, in 1984, Malcolm Marshall suffered a broken hand but came out to bat one-handed, determined not to abandon his partner. With his left arm in plaster, he even managed to thump a boundary. It wasn't the runs that mattered; it was the statement of defiance.

Steve Waugh provided another unforgettable example in the 2001 Ashes. With a torn hamstring, barely able to walk, he made a match-saving 157 not out at The Oval. Each hobble between the wickets drew applause. Waugh turned pain into inspiration, defining his reputation as Australia's iron man.

Careers Cut Short

Sometimes bravery wasn't enough. South African wicketkeeper Mark Boucher was forced into sudden retirement in 2012 when a bail ricocheted into his eye during a warm-up match. A freak accident, but one that ended a 15-year career in an instant.

The great fast bowler Shane Bond never had one catastrophic injury but was plagued by stress fractures and knee problems. He bowled with raw pace that thrilled crowds, but his body couldn't keep up. Eighteen Tests were all the world got; a career that might have been one of the greatest was reduced to a tantalising "what if."

Even the fittest weren't safe. Fielding genius Jonty Rhodes famously dislocated his shoulder in 1997 while diving, just one of many injuries that came from his fearless approach. He may have redefined fielding, but he paid for it in pain.

Women's Game, Same Sacrifices

Injuries in women's cricket carry the same weight and require the same courage. At the 2020 T20 World Cup, Ellyse Perry tore her hamstring and was ruled out of the tournament on home soil. It was a devastating blow for Australia's star all-rounder, but her absence only highlighted how much she meant to the team.

England's Sophie Ecclestone, the world's top-ranked T20 spinner, dislocated her shoulder in 2022, forcing her out of major matches. Even so, she returned to the top with her trademark calm precision, proof that resilience is as much a part of her game as spin.

Beth Mooney suffered a broken jaw in the nets just before the 2022 Ashes. Remarkably, she returned weeks later and top-scored in the World Cup final. Her comeback became a story of both bravery and brilliance.

Why These Injuries Matter

From Contractor's fractured skull to Hughes' tragic death, from Kumble's bandaged jaw to Mooney's broken face, injuries have shaped cricket's past and its future.

. They forced safety reforms: helmets, concussion rules, better medical care.

. They showed superhuman grit: bowlers and batters carrying on through pain.

. They ended careers too soon: Boucher, Bond, and others whose stories became cautionary tales.

. They inspired comebacks: Perry, Mooney, Dottin, proving resilience is as important as talent.

Cricket may be a sport of skill, elegance, and patience, but behind every highlight reel lies a human body pushed to its limit. The greatest injuries remind us that heroes are not just those who score centuries or take five-wicket hauls; sometimes they are the players who get back up, bruised and broken, but unbowed.

CHAPTER FOURTEEN: PRACTISING & NETS.

Every sport has its training ground, but in cricket, nothing quite matches the culture of "the nets." To outsiders, nets may look like nothing more than a few strips of turf caged in by mesh fencing. To cricketers, however, they are sacred spaces, where young beginners first learn how to hold a bat, where county pros sharpen their skills, and where international stars grind for hours in search of perfection.

What Are Nets?

. **Definition**: A cricket net is an enclosed practice area, usually a strip of turf, matting, or artificial surface, bounded by netting that prevents the ball from flying off in all directions.

. **Purpose**: Nets allow batters and bowlers to practise in a controlled environment. Bowlers can deliver without chasing the ball to the boundary; batters can hit without worrying about damaging cars or windows; coaches can stand alongside to give immediate feedback.

Nets are the laboratory of cricket. Out in the middle, there's nowhere to hide, but in the nets, players experiment with new grips, different stances, or wild variations.

The Outdoor Nets

Traditional nets are outdoors, usually on grass squares at clubs or schools.

. **Turf Nets**: These replicate match pitches. They require constant care from grounds staff and are used mainly by higher-level players. Batters get used to bounce, seam movement, and wear just as they would in a game.

. **Artificial Nets**: More common at grassroots level. They use synthetic matting rolled over a base, offering consistent bounce and durability. They are cheaper to maintain and can withstand heavy usage.

. **Caged Lanes**: Outdoor nets often consist of several lanes side by side, allowing multiple bowlers and batters to train simultaneously. These cages are community hubs. On summer evenings, the sound of leather on willow rings out as juniors, seniors, and veterans alike get their turn.

Outdoor nets have a culture of their own: the long queue of kids waiting for a bat; the teasing banter between friends; the bowler who swears the batter "would have been out" even though the edge just clipped the net.

The Rise of Indoor Nets

As cricket professionalised, indoor nets became essential. Modern facilities range from converted school gyms to purpose-built centres like the MCC Indoor Cricket Centre at Lord's.

. **Surfaces**: Usually matting or artificial turf designed to mimic outdoor conditions.

. **Bowling Machines**: A game-changer. These fire balls at set speeds, angles, and trajectories, allowing batters to hone their reflexes against simulated 90mph pace or looping spin.

. **Technology**: Some centres now use motion-tracking, video replay, and ball-flight analytics. Batters can review footwork in slow motion; bowlers can measure speed and spin instantly.

. **Accessibility**: Indoor nets keep cricket alive year-round. In England's damp winters, they allow players to train even when pitches outside are waterlogged.

Indoor nets are also great levellers. County professionals often share the same lanes with local club cricketers, schoolchildren, and weekend warriors, all battling against the same machine or coach's feed.

Why Nets Matter

1. Repetition and Muscle Memory
Cricket is a game of small margins. Nets allow the hundreds of repetitions needed to perfect a forward defence or yorker.

2. Confidence Building
For juniors, nets are safe spaces. Fear of getting out is removed, encouraging freedom to play shots.

3. Experimentation
International stars often talk about using nets to "fail safely." It's where innovations like the scoop, reverse sweep, or knuckleball were first attempted.

4. Team Bonding
Though individual in nature, nets bring teams together, bowlers trying to outthink batters, batters teasing bowlers, fielders chasing throwdowns.

Famous Stories from the Nets

· **Sachin Tendulkar**: As a boy, he would spend hours in Mumbai's Shivaji Park nets, sometimes batting until his coach physically dragged him out. He later said:

"The nets were my world. If I hadn't loved practice, I wouldn't have loved cricket."

- **Ellyse Perry**: The Australian great often speaks of her early memories in mixed junior nets, facing boys older and stronger than her. She credits those sessions with giving her resilience and fast reflexes.

- **Ben Stokes**: England's talisman, recalls smashing balls for hours in Durham's indoor nets as a teenager, developing the fearless hitting that defines his style.

- **Muttiah Muralitharan**: Teammates joked that he bowled more deliveries in the nets than some seamers did in matches. His endless practice loops honed the doosra that terrorised batters worldwide.

Nets at Grassroots Level

At the club level, nets are often the heartbeat of cricket. Juniors gather midweek for training, with volunteer coaches feeding balls, correcting stances, and teaching the etiquette of waiting your turn. Seniors use evening nets to sharpen up before weekend league fixtures.

. **Social Nets**: At some clubs, sessions are as much about catching up over a pint afterwards as they are about cricket.

. **Coaching Nets**: For youth development, structured drills in nets are vital, teaching young bowlers' accuracy, batters' shot selection, and everyone discipline.

Nets in the Professional Game

County and international teams use nets intensely, but with purpose. Unlike casual club sessions, pro nets are tailored:

. Batters face specific bowlers (pace or spin) to prepare for upcoming opponents.

. Bowlers target set lengths or deliveries, with immediate feedback from analysts.

. Fielding drills often run alongside, with slip catches or direct-hit practices fed from net edges.

During Test matches, nets become mini-theatres. Media hover, cameras roll, and journalists speculate based on who is practising. A batter in "the optional nets" is suddenly a headline.

Nets and the Spirit of Cricket

The net session is more than training. It's often where friendships are built, rivalries formed, and respect earned. For every child who plays professionally, there are thousands who simply remember the summer evenings they spent queuing with pads on, waiting for their few overs in the cage.

The net is cricket's hidden stage: unseen by crowds, but the place where games, careers, and dreams are built.

CHAPTER FIFTEEN: MATCH DAY – WHAT TO EXPECT

If you are playing your first ever match, then it's not as simple as just turning up and having a good day. There are many unknown, and sometimes 'unwritten', match day rules to follow:

Arrive Early

. Get to the ground with plenty of time before the match starts, usually 30–60 minutes early.

. This gives you time to find your changing room, get into your kit, and warm up without rushing.

Find Your Changing Room

. Most grounds have separate Home and Away changing rooms, ask someone from your team which is yours.

. Leave your things neatly so everyone has space.

Check Kit and Rules

. Make sure you have all your gear: bat, pads, gloves, helmet, box, spikes (if allowed).

Some clubhouses don't allow cricket spikes inside (they can damage floors). Always check signs or ask before walking in with spikes on; you may need to change shoes first.

Warm Up

. Do light stretches, gentle jogging, and some throwing or catching practice.

. Warm up your shoulders, hips, and legs to avoid injury.

Listen to the Captain's Plan

. The captain will explain the batting order, bowling plans, and field positions.

. Pay attention so you know your role from the start.

Respect Umpires and Opponents

. Accept the umpire's decisions without arguing, even if you disagree.

. Play hard but fair; shake hands before and after the match.

Enjoy the Day & Support Teammates

. Cheer for your team, help collect balls, and encourage players whether they do well or make mistakes.

. Stay involved even when you're not batting or bowling.

Cricket Teas

. In many UK club matches, there's a tea break halfway through the game (usually between innings).

. Expect sandwiches, cakes, biscuits, fruit, crisps, and plenty of tea/coffee.

. Everyone eats together; it's a social part of cricket, and a great time to chat and relax.

First Steps, First Nerves – Cricketers Remember Their Debuts

Every legend had to start somewhere. Yet first matches rarely go to plan. For some, they were a blur of nerves; for others, a comedy of errors; and for a few, an unexpected triumph that set the stage for greatness. These stories, from both men's and women's cricket, show the human side of cricketing beginnings.

Men's First-Match Memories

Sir Donald Bradman – Failure Before Immortality
1928, Australia vs England, Brisbane. A teenage Don Bradman, already whispered about as a prodigy, made just 18 and 1 on debut. The newspapers called him a disappointment. Bradman himself thought his chance had gone forever. Yet it was the making of him. He went away, rebuilt his game, and returned as the greatest batter in history.

Sachin Tendulkar – Blood on Debut
Aged just 16, Sachin walked out to face Pakistan's terrifying pace attack in 1989. A Waqar Younis bouncer smashed into his nose. Blood flowed, physios rushed on, but Sachin waved them away. "Main khelega" ("I will play"), he insisted. That refusal to quit defined his career: courage, grit, and sheer determination.

Andrew Flintoff – Empty Stomach, Full of Fire
Before his England debut in 1999, Flintoff was so nervous he couldn't eat breakfast. Once on the field, his nerves turned into fury; he smashed 50 off 40 balls. "I still don't know how I did it on no food," he later laughed.

Jimmy Anderson – Nearly Late for Lord's
On his 2002 debut, Anderson nearly missed the bus to Lord's thanks to London traffic. "I thought the captain would drop me before I'd even played," he admitted. He bowled with fire, dismissed Mark Vermeulen with his second ball, and the rest is history.

Ben Stokes – Fired Up and Fined
Stokes' ODI debut (2011 vs Ireland) was scrappy. He admitted nerves got the better of him, and he bowled several wides. Later, on his Test debut (2013 vs Australia), he was fined for swearing at Brad Haddin. "I was just too pumped up," he confessed. Today, that fire is his trademark.

Women's First-Match Memories

Charlotte Edwards – The Schoolgirl Captain
Picked for England at 16, Edwards turned up with her school packed lunch. "There I was, sat with my heroes, unwrapping cheese sandwiches." That humble start grew into a record-breaking career of 12,000+ international runs.

Sarah Taylor – "Do I Belong Here?"
On her 2006 debut, Taylor admitted she felt out of place. "I thought, I can't play at this level." But once the game began, she stumped a batter and realised: "Maybe I do belong." She went on to redefine wicketkeeping worldwide.

Heather Knight – The Broken Bat
On her debut tour, Knight realised she'd packed the wrong kit bag. She borrowed a teammate's bat and promptly snapped it in her first innings. "I was mortified," she recalled.

Smriti Mandhana – Teenage Star
Mandhana made her debut at 16 but admitted she was "terrified of forgetting the fielding positions." She calmed down by singing Bollywood songs to herself on the field. It worked; she scored 73 on Test debut.

Anya Shrubsole – "Don't Bowl a Wide"
On her first England game, Shrubsole was so nervous she kept whispering to herself: "Don't bowl a wide." Of course, her first ball was a wide. She laughed later: "At least it got better from there." Years later, she bowled England to a World Cup.

Why These First Matches Matter

The common thread in all these stories is not perfection; it's humanity. Even the best started with nerves, fumbles, or sheer chaos. For every young player out there, the nerves are normal. Mistakes are part of the journey. Even the greats began as rookies.

CHAPTER SIXTEEN: CRICKET ETIQUETTE AND SPIRIT OF THE GAME

Cricket isn't just about runs, wickets, and scoreboards. It's also about respect. From applauding a good shot, even when it's from the opposition, to knowing when not to wander behind the bowler's arm, etiquette is the glue that holds the spirit of the game together. Whether you're playing, umpiring, or simply watching from the boundary, understanding cricket's unwritten rules is just as important as knowing the written ones.

Captain Talks to the Umpire

. If there's a problem or a question about a decision, only the captain should speak to the umpire.

. The whole team crowding around looks disrespectful and can make things tense.

Avoid Swearing

. Keep language clean, even if you're frustrated. Swearing at opponents, umpires, or teammates is bad form and can lead to penalties.

Play Fair

. Follow the rules and don't try to cheat. This includes things like claiming a catch you didn't take cleanly.

Accept Decisions

. Once the umpire makes a decision, it's final, even if you think it's wrong. Arguing won't change it and can harm your team's reputation.

Celebrate Respectfully

. It's fine to cheer, high-five, and enjoy success, but avoid:

. Shouting in an opponent's face

. Mocking or taunting

. Over-the-top celebrations that delay the game

. The aim is to celebrate *with* your team, not *at* the opposition.

Look After the Pitch and Clubhouse

. **Pitch:** Don't damage the playing surface, avoid walking on it unnecessarily, don't dig spikes in, and repair any marks after bowling.

. **Clubhouse:** No muddy shoes indoors, respect furniture and facilities, and tidy up after yourself.

Leave the Ground Better Than You Found It

. Pick up litter, put equipment away, and help pack up. It's a sign of respect for the club and volunteers who run it.

Never Walk Behind the Bowler's Arm

One of the golden rules of cricket etiquette is never to walk behind the bowler's arm while they are running in. From the batter's perspective, the bowler is already charging in at speed, and their entire focus is locked on the ball. Any movement in the background, even something as small as a person strolling past, can be hugely distracting and potentially dangerous. This is why sight screens exist, giving the batter a still, clear backdrop, and why players, coaches, and spectators alike are expected to stay absolutely still until the ball is delivered. Once the ball is dead, it's safe to move again.

What is the Spirit of Cricket?

The Spirit of Cricket is the game's code of honour. It's about playing hard but fair, respecting everyone involved, and remembering that cricket is bigger than winning at all costs. It means showing courtesy to opponents, supporting your teammates, accepting the umpire's decisions, and protecting the traditions of the game. In short, **respect the game, respect others, and respect yourself**.

Beyond the Boundary – Cricket Etiquette and the Spirit of the Game

Cricket has been called many things: "a battle of patience," "organised loafing," "war without bullets." But above all, it has been called the *gentleman's game*. Yet its history shows that the true "spirit" has nothing to do with gender, class, or dress codes, and everything to do with fairness, respect, and honour. Across eras, famous cricketers have upheld, bent, or debated those unwritten rules, leaving stories that say as much about humanity as they do about cricket.

Yet this "spirit of cricket" is not a dusty relic. It has been lived, tested, and argued over in countless unforgettable moments. What follows are stories, some funny, some solemn, some fiery, that reveal how cricket's soul has been shaped on fields from Lord's to Lahore, Melbourne to Mumbai.

Adam Gilchrist Walks – 2003 World Cup Semi-Final

Sri Lanka were under pressure in the semi-final at Port Elizabeth. Gilchrist, in sublime touch, feathered an edge behind. The umpire's finger stayed down. Silence. Gilchrist looked up briefly, then tucked his bat under his arm and walked.

Commentators gasped. One said: *"You'll never see that again in a World Cup semi-final."* His captain Ricky Ponting later admitted he was stunned: "I wanted him to stay. But Gilly was always his own man."

Australia went on to win the tournament. But years later, fans remember the walk more than the hundreds. Gilchrist explained simply:

"The spirit of the game is more important than any trophy. If I knew I was out, I couldn't live with myself pretending otherwise."

Sarah Taylor's Bounce Call – Women's Ashes, 2009

In Worcester, Taylor dived forward to grab a chance off Australia's opener. England appealed, and the umpire raised the finger. Taylor instantly shook her head: "It bounced."

The batter survived, and Taylor's teammates patted her back. "That's Sarah," said Charlotte Edwards. "The wicket mattered less to her than the honesty."

That one moment was replayed on TV almost as much as her batting highlights. For many, it became proof that women's cricket embodied the spirit as much, if not more, than the men's game.

Jacques Kallis Calls Himself Out – 2001 India Tour

At Bangalore, Kallis nicked Anil Kumble faintly to the keeper. The umpire stayed unmoved, the Indians groaned, and Kallis walked. The crowd, normally hostile to visiting players, stood and applauded.

Rahul Dravid later said:

"It was rare to see someone give himself out in front of 40,000 people. That told me Kallis was as much a man of principle as he was a batsman of class."

When Spirit Clashed with the Law

Vinoo Mankad vs Bill Brown – 1947

At the SCG, Indian all-rounder Vinoo Mankad paused mid-delivery, noticing Bill Brown backing up too far. He whipped off the bails. Brown was out. The crowd booed; the press howled. "Ungentlemanly!" cried the headlines.

But Don Bradman himself defended Mankad:

"For the life of me, I cannot understand why he is being criticised. He did the right thing. The law is clear, and the batsman was at fault."

Thus, was born the word "Mankading," still dividing families in pub debates 75 years on.

Trevor Chappell's Underarm – 1981

A full house at the MCG. New Zealand needed six off the last ball. Greg Chappell, the Australian captain, told his younger brother Trevor: "Bowl it underarm."

Trevor did. The ball rolled tamely down the pitch, impossible to hit for six. The crowd jeered. Richie Benaud declared it "the most disgraceful thing I've ever seen." The Prime Ministers of both nations weighed in.

It was legal. But the spirit? Torn to shreds. The law was swiftly changed, but the scar remains: cricket's ultimate morality tale.

Controversy That Tested the Spirit

Alex Carey's Ashes Stumping – 2023

Jonny Bairstow wandered out of his crease after ducking a bouncer at Lord's. Alex Carey threw down the stumps and appealed. Out. The letter of the law said: "Yes!" The spirit? England fans erupted in fury. Members at Lord's heckled the Australians in the Long Room.

The Aussies stood firm: "It's in the laws." England's coach Brendon McCullum fumed: "We wouldn't want to win that way."

It became the most divisive "spirit" debate of the modern era, proving the argument is as alive today as in Mankad's time.

Charlotte Edwards – Respect as Captain

Edwards, England captain for a decade, was renowned for insisting her players applauded every opponent's milestone, fifty or hundred, no matter the match situation. "If you can't respect the opposition's effort," she said, "you don't deserve yours to be respected either."

Mithali Raj – "We Represent More Than Ourselves"

Raj famously said during the 2017 World Cup:

"We're not just playing for runs or wickets. We're showing young girls everywhere that they belong here too. That, to me, is the spirit of cricket."

Her leadership cemented the idea that etiquette is not only about opponents and umpires, but about carrying the hopes of millions with grace.

The Spirit in the Stands – Fans and Etiquette

The spirit of cricket isn't just lived on the pitch; it pulses through the stands. Cricket crowds are unique: part choir, part theatre troupe, part philosopher's club. They can make or break the atmosphere of a match, and sometimes even tip the balance of a contest.

Why the Spirit Still Matters

For all the controversy, comedy, and cultural spin, the spirit of cricket is still what makes the game unique.

In football, diving is routine. In rugby, brutality is expected. But in cricket, a batter walking, a bowler helping a rival up, or fans applauding an opponent's century still mean something.

CHAPTER SEVENTEEN- CRICKET SUPERSTITION FROM GRASSROOTS AND BEYOND.

Cricket Superstitions.

Cricket is already a game where someone in a white coat signals "four" by pretending to be an aeroplane, so it's hardly surprising that superstition thrives at the grassroots. But while the professionals have their odd habits (Steve Smith shadow-batting in the car park, anyone?), it's at the village green where things really get weird.

Take the sacred art of *boundary laps*. To the untrained eye, it's just someone stretching their legs. To the initiated, it's an act of sporting sorcery. Walk clockwise (left), and you're summoning runs as if you've got Ben Stokes on speed dial. Walk anticlockwise (right), and wickets tumble faster than you can say "dodgy hamstring." Woe betide the unsuspecting dog-walker who ambles the wrong way round mid-innings; suddenly it's their fault the opening bat's on 98 not out.

And the players aren't much better. Every club has a batter who refuses to wash his "lucky" socks (biological hazard by June), a bowler who insists the umpire's coin toss only works if he calls "heads," and a keeper who won't take his gloves off at tea because "they're just getting warm."

Spectators join in too. There's always one who swears the fate of the innings depends entirely on whether their camping chair faces square leg or cow corner. Another insists that if he nips to the loo, a wicket *always* falls. Entire batting collapses have been blamed on someone fetching a second pint from the bar.

Then there's the tea table ritual: apparently, Victoria sponge guarantees a batting collapse, while a custard slice is the surest sign of a century. Don't even ask what sausage rolls mean; it's complicated.

Do these superstitions work? Absolutely. Because when your team wins, you credit the lucky lap round the boundary. And when you lose, well, it's obviously because someone parked in the wrong spot.

That's the joy of grassroots cricket: a game played not just with bat and ball, but with ritual, routine, and just a sprinkle of nonsense. After all, when you're defending 114 on a Sunday afternoon, you'll take all the supernatural help you can get.

Rituals, Routines and Lucky Charms

Cricket has always balanced itself between the rational and the ridiculous, and the superstitions don't stop at grassroots level; they go all the way to the top. Here are some superstitions of international players, and they'd be the first to tell you if they didn't do these, then they wouldn't be up there as the world's greatest.

The Pads Come First

When Sachin Tendulkar padded up, the world watched. His batting was the most scrutinised event in India. Yet hidden from the cameras was his simplest of rituals: the left pad always went on before the right. He followed the routine without fail whether he was walking out at Wankhede Stadium or the MCG. Teammates knew not to disturb him while he went through the process.

Years later, Virender Sehwag told a story:
"Once, during a Test, someone hid Sachin's left pad by mistake. He was furious. He wouldn't wear the right until the left was found. We had to send a boy running around the pavilion. The moment he got it, Sachin calmed down and just said, 'Okay, I'm ready.' Then he went out and scored a hundred."

It wasn't just Tendulkar. Sunil Gavaskar, the great opener before him, believed in stepping onto the field right foot first. Even in the heat of the 1980s, facing the most dangerous West Indian fast bowlers, he refused to break the sequence. "If I got the right foot first, I knew I would survive," he once said.

And across the world, Australia's Ellyse Perry developed her own order-of-pads ritual. "Cricket is chaos," she explained, "but I can always control how I get dressed."

Steve Waugh's Red Hanky

Of all cricket's lucky charms, none is more famous than Steve Waugh's red handkerchief. It was given to him by his grandmother when he was a young cricketer, and it never left his pocket throughout his career.

The story goes that before the 1999 World Cup semi-final at Edgbaston, Waugh pulled it out in the dressing room, kissed it lightly, and stuffed it back before walking out to play one of the greatest innings of his life. That handkerchief became so famous that fans brought their own red rags into the stands, waving them whenever Waugh batted.

By the time Australia lifted the trophy at Lord's, the red hanky had become part of folklore. Waugh himself joked: "I never washed it too often. Maybe that's what scared the bowlers."

Smelly Socks, Sticky Gloves

Marcus Trescothick, England's left-handed opener, had a simple rule: never change your socks if you were scoring runs. His teammates both laughed and complained, because by the end of a long Test his socks were so rank that even the kit man refused to go near them.

But Trescothick swore by it. In the 2005 Ashes, he kept the same socks throughout the whole series. "They were practically walking on their own by the Oval Test," he admitted. But England won the urn, so who's to argue?

Ellyse Perry had her own version: in one Women's World Cup, she wore the same batting gloves all tournament. By the final, they were shredded, but Australia lifted the trophy and Perry finished Player of the Tournament. "You can't mess with what works," she laughed.

Jack Russell's Cold Tea

If superstition ever became performance art, it was with Jack Russell, England's eccentric wicketkeeper of the 1980s and 90s. His quirks filled entire books.

He drank cold tea from the same unwashed thermos flask year after year.

He ate baked beans every morning before play.

He slept with his cricket kit next to his bed.

He even refused to let his bats be cleaned, believing the old scuff marks brought him luck.

One journalist once described Russell's thermos as "the most feared object in English cricket." Yet Russell himself was unbothered: "The tea was just right, so why change it?"

Behind the eccentricity was something important: ritual kept him calm. As a wicketkeeper, waiting ball after ball, every tiny distraction mattered. His strange routines were his way of coping.

David Shepherd and the Nelson

Perhaps no superstition is more beloved by fans than umpire David Shepherd's hop at Nelson. For Shepherd, the score of 111, 222, or 333 was unlucky, "Nelson" in cricket slang. Whenever it appeared on the scoreboard, Shepherd would balance on one leg until the score moved on.

Crowds loved it. At the Oval in 1999, thousands of fans began hopping in unison with him when England's score reached 111. Even the players joined in, grinning as they batted. Shepherd chuckled: "Maybe I looked silly, but no one ever got out when I hopped."

His ritual became so iconic that whenever Nelson appeared, TV cameras would immediately cut to him. In that moment, superstition and theatre were one and the same.

Katherine Sciver-Brunt and the Chewing Gum

England fast bowler Katherine Sciver-Brunt (then Brunt) had one of the fiercest bowling run-ups in the women's game. But before she delivered her first ball, she would always chew the same brand of gum. If it wasn't available, she grew edgy, restless, even irritable.

"I don't know why," she admitted once. "It just settles me down. That first chew means I'm ready."

Her teammates began to notice that when Brunt's gum wasn't there, her temper flared. So, they kept emergency packets in the kit bag, "just in case." It became one of those unspoken rituals everyone respected.

Mithali Raj and the Necklace

India's legendary Mithali Raj, one of the most elegant batters in the women's game, always batted with a small necklace tucked inside her shirt. It wasn't jewellery for show; it was habit, comfort, and routine rolled into one.

She would touch it lightly before facing her first ball, a reminder of her roots and her parents' blessing. For Raj, the necklace wasn't about luck as much as *belonging*. "It keeps me grounded," she once said. "When I bat, I'm still that little girl from Hyderabad."

Steve Smith's Shadow Batting

Few modern cricketers are as ritualistic as Australia's Steve Smith. His fidgeting at the crease is notorious: tapping his bat, adjusting pads, scratching his guard, moving his shoulders. But his superstition begins even earlier.

Smith is known to "shadow bat" in hotel corridors, airports, even lifts. Once, during a rain delay at the SCG, he was spotted batting in the empty stairwell, complete with imaginary fielders. His teammates barely blinked; for Smith, this was normal.

"You've got to be obsessed to be great," said Justin Langer. "And Smudge is obsessed."

Shane Warne and the Zodiac

Shane Warne, who never quite trusted coaches or analysts, did trust astrology. He once revealed that he always checked his horoscope before big matches. "If it said something good, I felt bulletproof," he explained. If it didn't, he would find a way to spin it positively.

Teammates ribbed him mercilessly, but Warne shrugged: "Whatever gets you in the right headspace, mate." And when you've taken 700 Test wickets, maybe the stars really are on your side.

Shared Superstitions

Superstition in cricket is not always solitary; sometimes it spreads like wildfire. In the 2013 Women's World Cup, England's squad developed a ritual of sitting in the same bus seats every day. One day, a young player tried to switch spots, and the senior pros made her move back. "We're not tempting fate," Charlotte Edwards growled.

Similarly, during the 1999 World Cup, the South African team believed their dressing-room layout was lucky. When a cleaner rearranged the chairs before the semi-final, players hurried to put them back, muttering about "bad vibes." (They lost anyway, proof that superstition doesn't always save you.)

Why These Rituals Endure

Cricket, more than any other sport, is slow enough for the mind to wander. That's when doubts creep in. Superstitions fill the gap, offering control, comfort, or just the illusion of order. They may look odd to outsiders, but to players under the weight of expectation, they're part of survival.

As Jack Russell summed it up:
"People laugh at rituals. But when you're alone at the crease, with the whole world watching, sometimes that silly little thing is the only friend you've got."

CHAPTER EIGHTEEN: CRICKET SLANG AND WHAT IT MEANS.

ON THE FIELD:

Like every great sport, cricket has developed its own colourful language. A mix of tradition, humour, and insider shorthand that can leave newcomers scratching their heads. Learning the slang not only helps you follow the game, it also brings you into the club of those who speak cricket's secret code.

- **Sledging** – Verbal banter (sometimes cheeky, sometimes a bit rude) aimed at distracting or unsettling the batter.

- **Chin music** – A bouncer bowled close to the batter's head.

- **Jaffa / Peach** – An exceptionally good delivery that's very hard to play.

- **Yorker** – A ball bowled right at the batter's feet.

- **Bumper** – Another name for a bouncer.

- **Full toss** – A ball that reaches the batter without bouncing.

- **Beamer** – An illegal delivery that reaches the batter above waist height without bouncing.

- **Golden duck** – Getting out first ball faced.

- **Pair** – Getting out for 0 in both innings of a match.

- **Five-fer / Michelle** – A bowler taking five wickets in an innings ("Michelle" comes from actress Michelle Pfeiffer → "five-fer").

- **Ton** – 100 runs in a single innings.

- **Half-century** – 50 runs in a single innings.

- **Nurdle** – To gently guide the ball into gaps for runs, often with soft hands.

- **Play and miss** – Swinging at a ball and failing to hit it.

- **Leave** – Letting a ball go through to the keeper without playing at it.

- **Nick / Edge** – When the ball glances off the bat, usually caught behind.

Match & Tactics

- **Nightwatchman** – A lower-order batter sent in near the end of the day in a long match to protect better batters from having to bat in fading light.

- **Declaration** – When a captain ends the team's innings before all 10 wickets fall, usually to allow time to bowl out the opposition.

- **Follow-on** – In multi-day cricket, when the team batting second is forced to bat again immediately because they're so far behind on first innings runs.

- **Dead rubber** – A match that doesn't affect the overall series result.

- **Tailender** – A bowler who bats near the end of the order and isn't known for batting skill.

- **All-rounder** – A player good at both batting and bowling.

- **Sticky wicket** – Originally, a damp pitch making batting tricky; now also means a difficult situation.

In the Field

- **Cow corner** – An area on the leg side, often targeted for big slog shots.

- **Silly point / silly mid-on** – Close fielding positions with "silly" in the name because they're so close to the batter it's risky.

- **Plumb** – Obviously out (usually LBW).

- **Drop** – Failing to catch the ball.

- **Safe as houses** – Very reliable fielder.

Other Fun Ones

- **Baggy Green** – The famous cap given to Australian Test players; in England, the Test cap is just "England cap."

- **Beer match** – A friendly game, often after an official match, for fun.

- **Village** – Amateurish or low-standard play.

- **Sitter** – An easy catch that should be taken.

- **Rabbit** – A batter who's extremely poor against bowling.

- **Walking** – A batter choosing to leave the field without waiting for the umpire's decision after they know they're out.

CHAPTER NINTEEN: THE CRICKET DICTIONARY (A–Z)

Cricket, with its centuries of history and global reach, has collected a treasure trove of unique words, phrases, and expressions. Most are practical, describing techniques or positions on the field or terms about the game. This A–Z dictionary is your guide to the essential cricketing vocabulary, the perfect companion for anyone who's ever felt lost in the chatter from the commentary box or clubhouse.

All-rounder: A player strong at both batting and bowling.	**Leg bye:** Runs when ball hits the body (not bat).
Appeal: The fielding side's request to the umpire ('Howzat?') for a decision.	**Leg-side:** The side behind the batter's body; on-side.
Arm ball: A spinner's delivery that goes straight on without turning.	**Long-on/off:** Deep straight fielders near the boundary.
Around the wicket: Bowling from the opposite side of the stumps to change angle.	**Maiden over:** An over with no runs scored off the bat.
Ashes: Historic Test series between England and Australia.	**Mankad:** Run-out of the non-striker.
Back foot: Weight on the rear foot to play shorter balls.	**Middle order:** Batters who come in after the openers.
Backlift: The bat's backward movement before the swing forward.	**Nightwatchman:** Lower-order batter sent in late to protect a specialist.

Bail: One of two small pieces resting atop the stumps.	**No-ball:** Illegal delivery (overstep, beamer, etc.).
Bouncer: Short ball rising towards the batter's chest or head.	**Nets:** Practice lanes enclosed by netting.
Boundary: The field edge; also, a four or six scored.	**Obstructing the field:** Deliberately impeding fielders; results in dismissal.
Bowled: Ball hits stumps and dislodges bails.	**Off-break:** Spinner's ball turning from off to leg to a right-hander.
Byes: Runs when the ball misses bat and keeper.	**Off-side:** The side facing the bowler; opposite of leg side.
Century: 100 runs by a single batter.	**Over:** Six legal deliveries by one bowler.
Caught and bowled: Bowler catches a return catch from batter.	**Paddle sweep:** Gentle guiding sweep fine on the leg side.
Crease: Painted lines marking safe areas and bowling limits.	**Powerplay:** Fielding restriction periods in limited overs.
Cut shot: Square/off-side shot played with a horizontal bat.	**Playing on:** Batter deflects ball onto their own stumps.
Dead ball: Ball not in play; action has stopped.	**Quick:** A fast bowler.
Declaration: Ending an innings early in multi-day cricket.	**Reverse swing:** Late swing opposite to conventional direction.
Dot ball: A delivery with no run scored.	**Reverse sweep:** Sweeping shot played to the off-side with reversed grip.

Duck: Dismissal for zero runs.	**Run out:** Stumps broken before batter makes the crease.
Economy rate: Average runs conceded per over by a bowler.	**Run rate:** Average runs per over.
Edge: Contact off the side of the bat; can be caught.	**Seam:** Stitched ridge on a cricket ball.
Extras: Runs not off the bat: wides, no-balls, byes, leg-byes.	**Silly point:** Close, risky catching position on off-side.
Flipper: A spinner's ball that skids low after pitching.	**Slip:** Catching cordon next to the wicketkeeper.
Follow-on: Forcing the opposition to bat again immediately.	**Slog:** A big, high-risk shot.
Full toss: Ball reaches batter without bouncing.	**Square leg:** At right angles on the leg side.
Good length: Landing area that challenges the batter's judgment.	**Stumped:** Keeper removes bails with batter out of crease.
Googly: Leg-spinner's ball that turns the opposite way.	**Tail-ender:** Lower-order batter, usually a bowler.
Gully: Catching position between slip and point.	**Third man:** Deep fielder behind point on off-side.
Half-century: 50 runs by a single batter.	**Toss:** Coin flip deciding who bats/bowls first.

Hat-trick: Three wickets in three consecutive balls by a bowler.	**Umpire:** On-field official who makes decisions.
Hit wicket: Batter dislodges bails with bat or body.	**V:** Area straight down the ground for drives ('play in the V').
Hook shot: Aggressive shot to a short ball around head height.	**Wagon wheel:** Chart showing where a batter's runs were scored.
Innings: A team's or batter's turn to bat.	**Wicket:** Stumps/bails; a dismissal; or the pitch, context matters.
Inside edge: Ball takes the inner edge of the bat face.	**Wide:** Ball too wide or high to be fairly hit.
Jaffa: Slang for an unplayable ball.	**Wrist spinner:** Spinner using wrist (leg-spinner or left-arm unorthodox).
LBW: Leg before wicket; pad hit where ball would have hit stumps.	**Zooter:** A spinner's delivery that goes on with the arm (minimal turn). Also known as a back-spinner.

Hopefully now you'll have the tools to follow any match with confidence, whether it's a county clash at Headingley or an Ashes Test at Lord's. More than just jargon, cricket's vocabulary is part of its character: a living language that links generations of players and fans. Master these words, and you're not just watching cricket, you're speaking its very soul.

CHAPTER TWENTY: WHO SAID THAT? FAMOUS CRICKET QUOTES.

Cricket has always been more than runs and wickets; it's a game rich in wit, wisdom, and the occasional sledge that makes headlines. From the dry humour of commentators to the sharp retorts of players under pressure, cricket's quotes capture the spirit of the game in a way no scorecard ever could. This chapter brings together some of the most memorable lines ever spoken in and around the sport, words that have inspired, entertained, and sometimes even ruffled a few feathers.

On the Spirit of the Game

Cricket has always been about more than just runs and wickets. Many of the game's greatest figures have spoken about its character:

. *"Cricket is a game which the English, not being a spiritual people, have invented in order to give themselves some conception of eternity."* - **Lord Mancroft**

. *"You don't play for the crowd; you play for the country."* - **Mahendra Singh Dhoni**

On Technique and Talent

. *"Every ball went exactly where I wanted it to, until the batsman hit it."* - **Jim Laker**

. *"I always see the ball. I just close my eyes before it hits the bat."* - **Virender Sehwag** (half-joking).

. *"Don Bradman averaged 99.94. To me, he's 0.06 short of perfection."* - **Richie Benaud**

On Pressure and Performance

. *"To me, cricket is a simple game. Keep it simple and just go out and play."* - **Shane Warne**

. *"When you play test cricket, you don't give the Englishmen an inch. Play it tough, all the way. Grind them into the dust."* - **Allan Border**

. *"A true batsman should be in trouble at least once in a match."* - **Don Bradman**

Humour from the Commentary Box

Some of cricket's funniest lines have come not from players but from the commentary box:

. *"The bowler's Holding, the batsman's Willey."* - **Brian Johnston**, BBC, on Michael Holding and Peter Willey.

. *"The batsman's technique was like an old lady poking her umbrella at a wasp's nest."* - **John Arlott**

. *"And Glenn McGrath dismissed for two, just ninety-eight runs short of his century."* - **Geoffrey Boycott**

. *"The slow-motion replay doesn't show how fast the ball was really travelling."* - **Richie Benaud**

On English Cricket's Eternal Optimism

. *"We didn't lose the game; we just ran out of time."* - **Mark Taylor**

. *"It's not about losing the Ashes; it's about how badly you lose them."* - **David Lloyd**

Self-Deprecating Players

. *"Every cricketer knows that in the long run, he is to be bowled out."* - **Don Bradman**

. *"I bowl so slowly that if I don't like a ball, I can run after it and pick it up before it reaches the batsman."* - **Often attributed to Geoffrey Boycott (who loved repeating it), though variations pre-date him.**

. *"I've seen better batsmen in my kitchen playing with a rolling pin."* - **Freddie Trueman**

. *"The only exercise I get is when I walk to the crease to bat."* – **W.G. Grace**

Modern Funny Quips

. *"You don't win or lose the games because of the 11 you select. You win or lose with what those 11 do on the field."* - **Rahul Dravid**

. *"I knew I was in trouble when I saw the umpire's finger go up before the ball had even reached the wicketkeeper."* - **Andrew Flintoff**

. *"Sometimes it feels like I'm bowling to a barn door. Unfortunately, the barn door has wheels."* - **Graeme Swann**

Closing Thought

Few sports have produced as many quotable lines as cricket. From the philosophical to the ridiculous, the game has a way of inspiring both wisdom and wit. As John Arlott once said:

"Cricket is a reflection of life, but with more ducks."

PART TWO

CHAPTER TWENTY-ONE: FROM HUMBLE BEGINNINGS TO MODERN DAY

A Game in the Fields

The story of cricket begins not in grand stadiums or stately homes, but in the fields and commons of south-east England. The earliest references date to the 16th century, though the game was almost certainly played long before it appeared in written records.

The counties of Kent and Sussex are widely regarded as cricket's cradle. Here in the Weald, a region of thick forest, farmland, and sheep pastures, children and villagers improvised games with whatever was at hand. A crooked stick became a bat, a ball was crafted from rags, wool, or cork, and a sheep pen's gate or stool served as a target.

The name itself offers a clue. Scholars argue over whether "cricket" derives from the Middle Dutch *krick* (a stick), the Old French *criquet* (a club or stick), or the Anglo-Saxon *cricc* (a staff). Whatever its root, the word suggests something simple, wooden, and makeshift, a far cry from the polished willow and leather of today.

The First Written Traces

The earliest clear mention comes from 1597, in a legal case at Guildford, Surrey. A court record refers to "creckett" being played by schoolboys nearly 50 years earlier. This shows that cricket was already well enough established to be recalled as a childhood pastime of the mid-16th century.

In 1611, two men in Sussex were fined for playing cricket on a Sunday instead of attending church, evidence of both the game's popularity and the suspicion it aroused among the authorities. That same year, a dictionary defined "cricket" as "a boyish sport," underlining its image as a rustic diversion for the young.

From Village Green to Wagering Sport

By the 17th century, cricket had moved from casual play to more organised contests. Villages fielded teams, often drawing from the same families, and matches became festive community occasions. The game's simplicity was part of its appeal: it required little equipment, could be played on any patch of flat ground, and welcomed all ages.

It wasn't long before the gentry and nobility took notice. By the mid-1600s, cricket had become associated with gambling, a pastime in which wealthy patrons would sponsor teams, wager on results, and occasionally intervene to secure the services of talented players. Matches between counties such as Kent, Sussex, and Surrey became spectacles, watched by large crowds and bet upon heavily.

This period also saw cricket's first controversies. Puritan writers in the early 17th century frequently condemned cricket for distracting people from church. Several Sussex and Kent parish records show complaints about villagers playing cricket on Sundays rather than attending services. In 1646, a court case in Kent involved a wager over a cricket match, the first record of money being formally staked on the game.

The First Laws and the Rise of London Cricket

By the early 18th century, cricket was evolving into something recognisably close to today's sport. Matches were growing larger and more organised, attracting spectators from beyond the local community. The need for rules became obvious.

The first known Laws of Cricket were written in 1744. They specified the dimensions of the pitch, the weight of the ball, and the dismissal methods, bowled, caught, and run out. At this stage, bowlers delivered underarm, rolling or skimming the ball along the ground. Bats resembled curved clubs, designed more to sweep than to drive.

Meanwhile, London became the new hub of cricket. The Artillery Ground in Finsbury hosted many of the century's most famous matches, drawing aristocrats and commoners alike. Here, gambling on cricket reached fever pitch, with bets involving not just money but land, livestock, and even personal fortunes.

Hambledon: The First Cricket Club

The village of Hambledon in Hampshire holds a special place in cricket's history. In the 1760s and 1770s, the Hambledon Club emerged as the unofficial centre of the sport. Its matches against Kent, Surrey, and All-England elevens were widely reported, and innovations developed there, such as the straight bat, transformed play.

Hambledon's rise reflected cricket's transition from rustic amusement to structured sport. For the first time, players and spectators alike saw cricket as something with strategy, depth, and artistry.

The MCC and Lord's: Custodians of the Game

In 1787, a group of gentlemen founded the Marylebone Cricket Club (MCC) at Lord's in London. From this point onward, the MCC became the guardian of cricket's Laws, issuing the definitive code that governed the game worldwide.

Hayman, Francis (1708-1776) - The Royal Academy Cricket Club in Marylebone Fields, 1748

Cricket Across the Counties

As the 19th century began, county cricket flourished. Clubs in Surrey, Kent, Nottinghamshire, and Yorkshire grew powerful, producing legendary players such as W.G. Grace in the later Victorian era. Grace, with his flowing beard and towering presence, turned cricket into a national obsession. He combined showmanship with extraordinary skill, scoring runs in unprecedented volumes and drawing crowds of thousands.

County matches became formalised, and by 1890 the County Championship had begun. Cricket was now fully professionalised, with players contracted, statistics recorded, and newspapers reporting ball-by-ball accounts.

The Empire's Export

Cricket's expansion beyond England followed the routes of empire and migration. Soldiers, sailors, civil servants, and settlers carried the game abroad:

. **India**: Parsis in Bombay embraced cricket in the 1840s, later joined by Hindus, Muslims, and Europeans in tournaments such as the Quadrangular. The game became a unifying, and yet politically charged, arena.

. **Australia**: By the 1860s, English teams toured, and by 1877 the first official Test match was played in Melbourne. Australians soon proved they could match their former rulers.

. **The West Indies**: Cricket spread through plantations and clubs, later becoming a cornerstone of cultural pride.

. **South Africa**: The first South African Test was played in 1889, though against an under-strength England side.

. **New Zealand**: Cricket arrived with settlers and was formally established by the late 19th century.

By the end of the century, cricket had become global, though still tightly linked to imperial structures. It was at once a tool of colonial identity and a stage for colonised nations to assert themselves.

The Spirit and the Shadow

Even as cricket spread, it carried contradictions. It was a game of gentlemen and players, amateurs of noble birth and professionals of working-class origin. The amateur-gentleman divide lasted well into the 20th century, shaping cricket's culture and hierarchy.

It was also a game associated with fair play and sportsmanship, yet one where gambling, class tension, and colonial inequality were ever-present. For some, cricket represented the values of England; for others, it became a stage to challenge imperial authority.

Towards the Modern Era

By the dawn of the 20th century, cricket had laid its foundations:

. The Laws codified by the MCC.

. The County Championship defining domestic English cricket.

. The Ashes rivalry anchoring international contests.

. The spread of the game across the empire, giving rise to teams that would later challenge and surpass England.

From shepherd boys in Sussex fields to packed crowds at Lord's, cricket had grown into a national obsession and an imperial export. What began as a simple stick-and-ball pastime had become, by 1900, one of the world's most organised and symbolic sports, ready for the revolutions of the 20th century.

From Victorian Icons to the Global Game

The Age of Grace – Cricket's First Superstar

If the MCC provided cricket with its rules, it was W.G. Grace who gave it its soul. Born in 1848 in Gloucestershire, Grace grew into a figure so large that he seemed to stride across the game like a colossus. His bushy beard and commanding presence made him instantly recognisable; his batting feats made him unforgettable.

Grace scored over 54,000 first-class runs, including 126 centuries, numbers so astonishing for the time that they cemented his status as cricket's first celebrity. He also changed the way batting was approached: no longer was it just defensive prodding. Grace combined solidity with aggression, driving, cutting, and pulling with a style that brought the crowd to life.

The Victorians adored him. Crowds flocked by the thousands, newspapers followed his exploits, and he became a national hero. In many ways, Grace transformed cricket from a gentleman's pursuit into a mass spectator sport.

County Cricket and the Birth of the Championship

Alongside Grace's dominance came the formalisation of county cricket. By the mid-19th century, counties such as Surrey, Nottinghamshire, Kent, and Yorkshire had strong sides, often led by professional players. Matches between them became fiercely competitive, and spectators began to demand some kind of structure.

In 1890, the County Championship was officially created, with Surrey crowned the first champions. This gave English cricket a domestic backbone, ensuring that every summer brought a cycle of fixtures leading to a clear winner. The Championship would remain central to English cricket's identity well into the 20th century.

The Ashes are Born

Perhaps the most famous legend in cricket emerged in 1882. England, the dominant power, suffered a shock defeat to Australia at The Oval. The *Sporting Times* printed a mock obituary for English cricket, declaring that "the body will be cremated and the ashes taken to Australia."

When England toured Australia later that year, captain Ivo Bligh was presented with a small urn, supposedly containing the ashes of English cricket. Thus began the Ashes rivalry, which became the heartbeat of international cricket. The Ashes symbolised more than just sport: it was England's pride against the colony's defiance, a contest rich in drama, tension, and mutual respect.

The Gentlemen and the Players

Throughout the 19th century, cricket was shaped by its class divide. The "Gentlemen" (amateurs from wealthy backgrounds) were often captains, even if they weren't the best players. The "Players" (professionals, usually working-class) were paid to play but rarely given the same respect.

This divide was embodied in the annual Gentlemen v Players match, staged from 1806 to 1962. Though presented as a festival, it also highlighted cricket's inequalities. A professional like Wilfred Rhodes or Jack Hobbs could outshine the amateurs yet still defer to them socially.

The Early 20th Century – A Game in Transition

As the 20th century dawned, cricket was flourishing. Test cricket had taken root between England, Australia, and South Africa. County cricket thrived. But change was on the horizon.

One of the first true modern batsmen was Sir Jack Hobbs of Surrey, nicknamed "The Master." Hobbs combined technical brilliance with immense consistency, scoring a world-record 61,760 first-class runs and 199 centuries. He became a symbol of reliability during the turbulent years of the First World War and after.

Alongside Hobbs, bowlers such as Sydney Barnes emerged as innovators, experimenting with swing, seam, and spin to devastating effect. Cricket was becoming more scientific, more professional, more advanced.

The Bradman Era

No history of cricket can omit Sir Donald Bradman, the Australian who redefined batting. Born in 1908, Bradman dominated the interwar and postwar game like no one before or since. His career average of 99.94 in Test cricket remains one of the most astonishing statistics in any sport.

Bradman was not only a cricketer but a symbol. In Depression-era Australia, he represented hope and resilience. His runs lifted spirits during hard times, and his duels with England's bowlers became matters of national pride. The notorious Bodyline series of 1932–33, when England's fast bowlers targeted him with leg-side short-pitched deliveries, nearly caused a diplomatic incident. Cricket had never been so politically charged.

War and Aftermath

Both World Wars disrupted cricket profoundly. Many players enlisted; some never returned. But cricket also became a symbol of endurance. Matches continued in reduced form, offering respite from turmoil.

After 1945, cricket had to rebuild. England found a new hero in Sir Len Hutton, the first professional to captain the national side, a landmark in breaking down class barriers. Hutton's stoic batting helped restore stability.

In the 1950s, the West Indies began to rise, led by dazzling talents like Frank Worrell, Everton Weekes, and Clyde Walcott, the famous "Three Ws." They brought flair, joy, and a sense of Caribbean pride to the game.

The Post-War Expansion of Test Cricket

By the mid-20th century, the map of Test cricket was expanding rapidly:

. **India** had joined the fold in 1932.

. **Pakistan** emerged in 1952, quickly proving themselves formidable.

. **The West Indies** developed into world-beaters.

. **New Zealand** and **later Sri Lanka** found their footing.

Cricket was no longer just England's sport; it was becoming the shared property of many nations, each bringing its own style and spirit.

Towards the Modern Professional Game

By the 1960s, cricket faced challenges. Audiences were shrinking, matches were long, and television demanded excitement. This led to the birth of limited-overs cricket. In 1963, the first one-day county competition was launched in England. The format proved popular, and within a decade the first One-Day International (ODI) was played in 1971.

The 1970s also brought drama off the field. Australian media mogul Kerry Packer launched World Series Cricket in 1977, breaking away from cricket's establishment. Players were suddenly paid properly, matches featured coloured clothing, white balls, floodlights, and television spectacle. What was once considered heresy became the norm, and cricket was never the same again.

By the close of the 20th century, cricket had completed a profound transformation. It had started as a rural game of sticks and stones, grown into a Victorian obsession under Grace, been dominated by Bradman's genius, and finally turned into a modern, professional, global sport.

Key Figures of the 19th & 20th Century

. **W.G. Grace** – turned cricket into a national spectacle.

. **Jack Hobbs** – "The Master," record-breaking run-scorer.

. **Donald Bradman** – cricket's greatest batsman.

. **Len Hutton** – broke class barriers as England's first professional captain.

. **Frank Worrell** – first great West Indies leader, embodying dignity and pride.

. **Kerry Packer** – changed cricket's economics and entertainment forever.

A New Century, A New Game

The Arrival of T20 – Cricket's Revolution

As the 20th century ended, cricket was already professional, televised, and global. But the new century brought an innovation that would change everything: Twenty20 cricket.

The format was first trialled in England in 2003 by the ECB, designed to fit neatly into an evening, three hours of entertainment, fast-paced, family-friendly.

By 2007, the first ICC World T20 was staged in South Africa. The final between India and Pakistan in Johannesburg drew a global audience in the tens of millions, signalling that cricket had found its 21st-century blockbuster.

The Indian Premier League – A Sporting Superpower

If T20 was cricket's spark, the Indian Premier League (IPL) was its explosion. Founded in 2008, the IPL combined Bollywood glamour, corporate money, and cricketing talent from around the world.

City-based franchises such as the Mumbai Indians, Chennai Super Kings, and Kolkata Knight Riders became household names. Players were auctioned for millions, cheerleaders danced at the boundaries, and cricket turned into prime-time theatre.

At first, some feared this would dilute Test cricket. But the IPL proved too powerful to resist. It gave young Indian cricketers exposure, brought legends like Shane Warne and Sachin Tendulkar together with rookies, and redefined what a cricketer could earn. It wasn't just a league; it was a cultural phenomenon.

Other nations soon followed, the Big Bash League in Australia, the Caribbean Premier League, the Pakistan Super League, and many more. T20 leagues spread like wildfire, giving cricket fans year-round entertainment.

The Hundred – England's Gamble

While T20 exploded globally, the ECB decided to push innovation further with The Hundred, launched in 2021. Each team faces just 100 balls, bowlers deliver either 5 or 10 at a time, and matches are even shorter than T20s.

The Rise of Women's Cricket

Perhaps the most important development of the modern era has been the rise of women's cricket.

Though women had been playing since the 18th century, it was only in the late 20th and early 21st century that they began to receive serious recognition.

. The Women's World Cup actually pre-dates the men's, first staged in 1973, two years before the men's version.

. England and Australia dominated early on, but in the 21st century, nations like India, South Africa, and New Zealand emerged as forces.

. The 2017 Women's World Cup Final at Lord's drew a capacity crowd and millions of TV viewers, as England defeated India in a thriller.

. Today, stars such as Ellyse Perry, Heather Knight, Smriti Mandhana, and Harmanpreet Kaur inspire girls worldwide.

The introduction of professional contracts in England, Australia, and India has transformed women's cricket from amateur to elite. The launch of leagues like the Women's Big Bash League and Women's Premier League (India, 2023) has made women's cricket a prime-time product in its own right.

Test Cricket – The Old Guard Holds On

Amid all this change, Test cricket, the oldest format, remains the pinnacle for many players. Matches like the Ashes 2005 series in England, or India's stunning victory at the Gabba in 2021, proved that five-day cricket still provides drama unmatched by any other sport.

Yet, Test cricket faces challenges. Crowds are smaller, attention spans shorter, and boards often prioritise shorter formats for financial reasons. Still, its prestige remains intact: a century at Lord's, or a five-wicket haul at the MCG, is still the ultimate dream.

Technology and the Modern Game

Modern cricket is also defined by its embrace of technology.

. The Decision Review System (DRS), introduced in 2008, allows players to challenge umpiring calls using ball-tracking and snickometer replays.

. High-definition broadcasts and data analytics have reshaped how fans watch and how teams prepare.

. Social media gives players direct connections with fans, making stars like Virat Kohli, Ben Stokes, and Ellyse Perry global icons.

Even equipment has changed: bats are bigger, protective gear lighter, and the modern cricketer is a fitter, faster, more explosive athlete.

Cricket in the Olympics and Beyond

For much of its history, cricket was absent from the world's greatest sporting stage, the Olympics. But in 2028, cricket will return to the Games in Los Angeles as a T20 format. This promises to open the sport to new audiences and nations.

Cricket is also spreading to unexpected places. The United States now has Major League Cricket (MLC), with big-name players joining American franchises. Afghanistan, once a war-torn nation with little cricketing heritage, has become a powerhouse in T20 thanks to stars like Rashid Khan. Ireland has full Test status. The game is bigger and broader than ever.

CONCLUSION – A GLOBAL, MULTI-FORMAT FUTURE

From the shepherd boys of medieval England to the floodlit stadiums of Mumbai and Melbourne, cricket has travelled an extraordinary journey. It has adapted, innovated, and reinvented itself time and again:

. **Tests** still embody tradition and ultimate skill.

. **ODIs** remain global showpieces with their World Cup spectacle.

. **T20s** deliver entertainment and drama in three hours flat.

. **The Hundred** and future formats may yet push boundaries further.

. **Women's cricket** has finally claimed its rightful place alongside the men's game.

. **Disability cricket** proves the game truly is for everyone.

What began as a rustic pastime is now a global sport watched by billions. And yet, its essence is unchanged: bat versus ball, skill versus skill, a contest where pride, patience, and passion still mean everything.

CHAPTER TWENTY-TWO. THE HISTORY OF MEN'S CRICKET: FROM VILLAGE GREENS TO GLOBAL ARENAS.

Beginnings on the Greens

By the late 1600s, cricket was well established in Kent, Sussex, and Surrey, where it drew in both farm labourers and local gentry. The seeds of its future popularity were already sown in these early village rivalries.

The 18th Century – Patrons and the Rise of Professionalism

As the 18th century dawned, cricket began to move beyond parish recreation into a structured sport. A key driver was gambling. Wealthy landowners wagered heavily on the outcomes of matches and began hiring skilled cricketers from rural communities.

The age of the patron saw noblemen such as the Duke of Richmond in Sussex and Sir Horace Mann in Kent assemble elevens to play against rival aristocrats. They employed talented local men, farmers, shepherds, carpenters, who became the first professional cricketers, paid retainers to work on estates but valued most for their cricketing ability.

It was in this atmosphere that cricket first produced recognisable stars. Richard Newland of Slindon became England's earliest celebrated batsman, while Edward "Lumpy" Stevens of Surrey earned a reputation as the most accurate bowler of his age. His accuracy exposed flaws in the two-stump wicket, prompting the addition of a third in 1775, a landmark in the game's development.

The period also saw cricket clubs take root. Most famous was Hambledon Club in Hampshire. Though rural in setting, Hambledon became a powerhouse, producing legendary players such as John Small, whose straight bat technique revolutionised batting, and Thomas Brett, among the finest bowlers of his generation.

The 19th Century – Laws, Counties, and the Dawn of International Cricket

By the early 19th century, cricket had grown into a national obsession in England. The first codified Laws had been published. These were refined and expanded over time, ensuring uniformity as cricket spread across the country.

The game itself was evolving quickly. Bowling, once exclusively underarm, shifted first to round-arm deliveries, pioneered by Kent's John Willes, and eventually to overarm, legalised in 1864. This innovation transformed cricket, empowering bowlers and forcing batters to develop new techniques.

Meanwhile, county sides were taking shape. Sussex founded the first official county club in 1839, with Nottinghamshire and Kent following soon after. By 1890, the County Championship was formally established, creating a competitive domestic structure that underpinned the sport.

Photo by E. Hawkins and Co., Brighton.

C. J. Kortright.   J. R. Mason.   A. C. Maclaren.   J. A. Dixon.   West, Umpire.
S. M. J. Woods.   A. E. Stoddart.   W G. Grace.   C. L. Townsend.   F. S. Jackson.
Captain Wynyard.   G. MacGregor.

GENTLEMEN V. PLAYERS

(Played at Lord's).

W. G. GRACE'S JUBILEE, JULY 1898.

This century also gave rise to a pantheon of legendary players:

. **Fuller Pilch**, whose forward defensive stroke shaped batting technique.

. **Alfred Mynn**, the "Lion of Kent," renowned for his powerful all-round displays.

. **William Clarke**, founder of the All-England Eleven touring team, which spread cricket's popularity to new audiences.

Most influential of all was W.G. Grace. Towering, bearded, and larger than life.

The 19th century also marked the dawn of international cricket. In 1877, England played Australia in Melbourne in the first official Test match. Five years later, the Ashes rivalry was born after Australia's famous victory at The Oval in 1882 prompted a satirical obituary declaring the "death of English cricket." The urn that followed became the game's most iconic trophy.

The 20th Century – Icons and Expanding Horizons

The 20th century began with cricket firmly embedded as England's summer game and increasingly international. New Test nations joined: South Africa (1889), West Indies (1928), New Zealand (1930), and India (1932).

Cricket now had heroes to match its global reach.

. **Jack Hobbs**, "The Master," scored more than 61,000 runs and 197 centuries, setting records that may never be surpassed.

. **Herbert Sutcliffe**, his partner, formed England's most dependable opening pair.

. **Donald Bradman**, "The Don," towered over the sport with a Test average of 99.94, inspiring a Depression-weary Australia and becoming a symbol of national pride. His dominance forced England into the controversial Bodyline series of 1932–33, where bowlers targeted the body to curb his run-scoring.

After World War II, cricket helped bring nations together. The West Indies, with players like the Three Ws - Weekes, Walcott, and Worrell, established themselves as a force. Len Hutton became the first professional to captain England. India and Pakistan's rivalry added new intensity to the Test arena.

By the 1970s, the sport shifted again. The introduction of One-Day Internationals (ODIs) in 1971, followed by the inaugural World Cup in 1975, revolutionised cricket. The shorter format demanded new tactics, greater aggression, and dynamic fielding. Charismatic players like Ian Botham, Kapil Dev, and Viv Richards embodied the bold new era.

The 1980s saw the West Indies dominate world cricket with their fearsome fast-bowling quartets and swaggering batting. By the 1990s, cricket was a truly global spectacle, producing icons such as Sachin Tendulkar, Brian Lara, Shane Warne, and Wasim Akram.

The 21st Century – A Global Game

The 21st century brought both continuity and upheaval. Test cricket remained the pinnacle for purists, but limited-overs cricket surged in popularity. The launch of the Twenty20 format in 2003, and especially the Indian Premier League (IPL) in 2008, transformed the sport's economics. Cricketers became global celebrities, earning fortunes and gaining followings beyond national borders.

Modern greats carried the torch:

- **Ricky Ponting, Glenn McGrath, and Adam Gilchrist dominated for Australia.**

- **MS Dhoni** and **Virat Kohli** elevated India into a cricketing superpower.

- **Ben Stokes** and **Joe Root** revived England's fortunes with unforgettable performances, including the 2019 World Cup triumph.

The men's game today straddles formats, the endurance of Tests, the strategy of ODIs, and the thrill of T20s. It is a sport with ancient roots but a thoroughly modern reach, broadcast to billions from Melbourne to Mumbai.

CONCLUSION – THE JOURNEY OF MEN'S CRICKET

From its rustic beginnings on English village greens to the billion-dollar stadiums of today, men's cricket has undergone a transformation unlike any other sport. It has been shaped by farmers and aristocrats, patrons and professionals, amateurs and superstars. It has endured wars, colonial shifts, and the challenges of modern entertainment, yet its essence, duels between bat and ball over 22 yards, remains timeless.

Men's cricket is not simply a game; it is a living history, a thread running from the sheep-grazed commons of Tudor England to the roaring stands of the MCG and Eden Gardens. And its story, still being written, carries the weight of centuries on every delivery bowled.

The early pioneers - from village heroes like Richard Newland, to Hambledon strategists like John Small, to global icons like W.G. Grace - built the bedrock of cricket as we know it. They turned a rustic English pastime into a sport of structure, spectacle, and worldwide reach.

CHAPTER TWENTY-THREE: THE HISTORY AND FACES OF WOMEN'S CRICKET

The England Women's Cricket Team touring Australia and New Zealand, 1934-1935

Early Beginnings (18th Century)

The first recorded women's cricket match took place in 1745 in Surrey, between Bramley and Hambledon. Players reportedly wore dresses and caps decorated with ribbons, and hundreds gathered to watch. The teams were made up of farm labourers and village women, competing for wagers and local pride.

Through the late 18th and early 19th centuries, women's matches continued sporadically. In 1777, a Sussex game drew thousands, showing the appetite for female cricket as a form of community entertainment. However, players' names were rarely recorded, reflecting the dismissive attitude of the press.

Victorian Foundations (19th Century)

By the 1880s, women's cricket was starting to formalise. The most important development was the creation of the White Heather Club in Yorkshire in 1887 - one of the first organised women's clubs in the world.

The White Heather Club was founded by aristocratic women, including:

. The Hon. M. Brassey

. The Hon. Beatrice Brassey (later Stacey)

. Lady Milner

. Lady Idina Nevill (later Lady Idina Brassey)

. Lady Henry Nevill

. The Hon. Maud Lawrence

. Miss Chandos-Pole

. Miss Street

They adopted pink, white, and green club colours, wore long skirts and wide-brimmed hats, and toured across England. Matches were sometimes treated as novelties, but their skill soon won respect.

Lucy Ridsdale (later Lady Lucy Baldwin) was one of their best batters, averaging 62 runs in 1892 and scoring 53 at Osmaston in 1896. Other notable members included **Dorothy and Sylvia Heseltine,** who later founded teams in Hampshire and Buckinghamshire, and **Nona Hermon-Worsley,** who produced a match-winning performance of 73 runs and 7–38 in 1935.

White Heather fixtures included playful "Married vs Single" games as well as serious contests, such as their annual Oxfordshire matches from 1908 against Miss Evelyn Tubb's XI. By keeping fixtures regular, they gave women cricketers structure long before national organisations existed.

The club eventually dissolved in 1957, but its impact was profound: it normalised women's cricket as a serious pursuit, inspired generations in Yorkshire, and provided role models decades before professional pathways.

Interwar Growth (20th Century Pioneers)

The Women's Cricket Association (WCA) was founded in 1926, providing the first national structure. With it came tours, county matches, and the beginning of international cricket.

Key figures included:

· **Betty Archdale (1907–2000)**: barrister, suffragist, and England's first Test captain in 1934.

· **Myrtle Maclagan (1911–1993)**: opening batter and bowler; scored 119 in the first ever women's Test (1934) and took 5 wickets in the same game.

· **Mollie "The Demon" Hide (1913–1995)**: captain of England from 1937 to 1951, known for her determination and leadership.

In 1934, England beat Australia in the first official women's Test, creating the Women's Ashes rivalry. By 1935, New Zealand had joined the Test fold.

Post-War to the 1970s

After World War II, women's cricket continued but with limited funding and recognition. The sport relied heavily on players' own resources.

The defining pioneer of this period was **Rachael Heyhoe Flint (1939–2017).**

. England captain from 1966-1977.

. Led England to win the 1973 Women's World Cup (the first ever World Cup in cricket, men's or women's).

. Campaigned for sponsorships and MCC membership for women.

. Later became the first woman on the MCC Committee and a life peer.

. Inducted into the ICC Hall of Fame (2010).

Her charisma and campaigning transformed the sport's visibility.

Yorkshire's Powell Twins

In the 1970s and 80s, Jane and Jill Powell represented England.

· Jane became a coach, sports educator, and later the first female President of Yorkshire County Cricket Club in 2022, during a time of institutional reform.

· Jill's career was shorter, but the twins were symbols of Yorkshire's contribution to women's cricket.

The Professional Era (21st Century)

· **1998**: the WCA merged into the ECB, uniting men's and women's cricket.

· **2009**: the first ICC Women's World T20 signalled the rise of the short format.

· **2014**: central contracts were introduced in England, professionalising the sport.

· **2015**: Australia's Women's Big Bash League (WBBL) launched.

· **2017**: the Women's World Cup final at Lord's drew 26,000 fans, millions on TV, and confirmed women's cricket's mainstream status.

· **2021**: The Hundred debuted, giving equal billing to men's and women's fixtures.

· **2023**: India launched the Women's Premier League (WPL), the richest women's cricket competition to date.

Modern Heroes

England: Heather Knight, Nat Sciver-Brunt, Katherine Sciver-Brunt, Sophie Ecclestone, Danni Wyatt.

Australia: Ellyse Perry, Meg Lanning, Alyssa Healy.

India: Mithali Raj, Jhulan Goswami, Smriti Mandhana.

West Indies: Stafanie Taylor.

Pakistan: Sana Mir.

New Zealand: Suzie Bates.

These players are household names and role models, unimaginable to pioneers like White Heather.

Timeline of Women's Cricket

- 1745 – First recorded women's match (Bramley vs Hambledon, Surrey).
- 1777 – Women's match in Sussex attracts thousands.
- 1887 – White Heather Club founded, Yorkshire.
- 1892 – Lucy Ridsdale averages 62 for White Heather.
- 1896 – Lucy Ridsdale scores 53 at Osmaston.
- 1908 – Annual White Heather vs Miss Evelyn Tubb's XI fixtures begin.
- 1926 – Women's Cricket Association founded.
- 1934 – First women's Test (England beat Australia).
- 1935 – New Zealand women's first Test.
- 1958 – International Women's Cricket Council founded.
- 1973 – First Women's World Cup (England win).
- 1976 – India women's first Test.

- 1998 – WCA merges with ECB.

2009 – First ICC Women's World T20.

- 2014 – England introduce central contracts.

- 2015 – Women's Big Bash League begins.

- 2017 – World Cup final at Lord's: 26,000 crowd.

- 2021 – The Hundred launches with equal billing.

- 2023 – Women's Premier League (WPL) launched.

Key Pioneers

Early: White Heather Club (Brassey sisters, Lady Milner, Lucy Ridsdale, Dorothy & Sylvia Heseltine, Nona Hermon-Worsley).

Interwar: Betty Archdale, Myrtle Maclagan, Mollie Hide.

Post-war: Rachael Heyhoe Flint.

Modern Yorkshire: Jane & Jill Powell.

Today: Heather Knight, Sophie Ecclestone, Ellyse Perry, Smriti Mandhana, Stafanie Taylor, and many others.

CHAPTER TWENTY-FOUR: DISABILITY CRICKET AND ITS PIONEERS

Disability Cricket – From Improvised Games to Global Glory

Beginnings in Sound and Silence

The story of disability cricket begins in two very different summers. In Sussex in the 1880s, a group of deaf cricketers founded one of the earliest Deaf Cricket Clubs. At a time when deaf people were often marginalised, cricket became a way for the community to come together, compete, and prove that the game could belong to them as much as anyone else.

Half a world away, in the 1920s Melbourne, two blind factory workers filled a tin can with stones and began rolling it to each other so they could hear the "ball." What began as a workplace diversion grew into the first version of blind cricket. These improvised beginnings, one shaped by silence, the other by sound, planted the seeds of what would become a global movement.

Blind Cricket: From Tin Cans to World Cups

By the 1940s and 50s, blind associations in Britain were organising matches, often using improvised equipment such as football rattles or bottle tops inside balls. In the 1970s and 80s, organisers like George Ferguson began to standardise blind cricket in the UK, while in India, George Abraham founded the World Blind Cricket Council in the 1990s.

The breakthrough came in 1998 with the inaugural Blind Cricket World Cup in Delhi. England's blind cricketers travelled to India and, against the odds, lifted the trophy, one of the proudest moments in the country's disability sporting history. Since then, India and Pakistan have often dominated, but England remains a strong force, reaching multiple finals and semi-finals.

Hero: *Luke Sugg*, one of England's most accomplished blind players, summed up the pride:

"Blind cricket isn't a second-class game. It's the same passion, the same drive, the same pride in pulling on that England shirt."

Deaf Cricket: The Oldest Tradition

Deaf cricket has the longest roots, dating back to the Victorian era. Sussex Deaf Cricket Club, founded in the 1880s, was one of the first of its kind, and by the 20th century deaf sides were competing regularly across England.

The England Deaf team now competes in World Cups and bilateral series against Australia, India, and South Africa. One of its most inspirational captains, Umesh Valjee, earned an MBE for services to the game. He described cricket's unique power:

"On the field, it doesn't matter whether you can hear or not. It's just you, your bat, the ball, and your team. Cricket gave me equality before the world gave me rights."

England Deaf teams have recorded notable victories, including series wins against South Africa and strong performances at World Cups.

Learning Disability (LD) Cricket: A Game for All

Learning Disability cricket emerged more recently, in the 1980s and 90s, as changing social attitudes recognised the right of people with intellectual disabilities to play competitive sport. The English Federation of Disability Sport (EFDS) and the ECB helped establish county programmes, leading to the first national England LD team in 2005.

The defining moment came a decade later, when Chris Edwards captained England to victory in the 2015 Tri-Series in Australia, beating the hosts and South Africa. He reflected:

"We weren't just playing for ourselves; we were proving what people with learning disabilities can achieve when given the chance."

Physical Disability (PD) Cricket: Strength in Adaptation

Physical Disability cricket took shape in the late 1990s, with charities and local clubs staging matches for players with limb differences, cerebral palsy, and joint conditions. With ECB backing in the 2000s, it developed into an elite pathway.

The breakthrough came in 2015 when England won the inaugural PD World Cup in Bangladesh, defeating Pakistan. They repeated the feat in 2019 at Worcester, beating India in front of jubilant home crowds.

Heroes of PD Cricket:

- *Callum Flynn*, a cancer survivor, became one of England's star batsmen:

"When I walk out to bat, I'm not a cancer survivor. I'm just an England cricketer."

- *Liam Thomas* became famous worldwide when his prosthetic leg came off mid-fielding, and he simply carried on chasing the ball. His grit embodied the spirit of disability cricket.

Table Cricket: Heroes in Classrooms

Not all disability cricket takes place on full pitches. In the 1990s, Doug Williamson at Nottingham Trent University created Table Cricket, played on a table tennis table with ramps and panels. Adopted by the Lord's Taverners, it spread across schools and community hubs, giving young people with profound disabilities the chance to compete.

Each year, county heats lead to a national final at Lord's, a moment of glory at the Home of Cricket. Williamson's vision was simple:

"We wanted a game where no child was left on the sidelines. Table Cricket makes heroes in classrooms, not just stadiums."

Today, Table Cricket reaches over 10,000 children annually and has spread internationally to countries including India, South Africa, and Australia.

The National Pathway and International Stage

All disability formats now sit under the ECB Disability Cricket Pathway, which guides players from grassroots to elite level. County boards such as the Yorkshire Cricket Board run local programmes, while national squads compete in international tournaments.

In 2022, the ECB launched the Disability Premier League (DPL), bringing together the best PD and LD players in mixed squads. With live-streamed matches and growing media coverage, the DPL represents a new era of professionalism and visibility.

Globally, the movement is coordinated by:

- **World Blind Cricket Council (Blind World Cups).**
- **Deaf International Cricket Council (Deaf World Cups).**
- **ICC Disability Committee** (LD and PD formats).

Major nations include India, Pakistan, Australia, South Africa, Sri Lanka, Bangladesh, and England.

England's Greatest Achievements

- **Blind Cricket** – World Cup champions, 1998 (Delhi).
- **Deaf Cricket** – Series victories against South Africa and India.
- **Learning Disability** – Tri-Series champions, 2015 (Australia).
- **Physical Disability** – World Cup champions, 2015 (Bangladesh); Tri-Series winners, 2019 (Worcester).

· **Table Cricket** – Ongoing national finals at Lord's, with thousands of participants every year.

CONCLUSION – A GAME FOR ALL

From the tin can in a Melbourne factory to the roar of a World Cup final, disability cricket has travelled an extraordinary journey. Each adaptation. Blind, Deaf, Learning Disability, Physical Disability, and Table Cricket are rooted in resilience, ingenuity, and the refusal to accept exclusion.

Today, whether it is a blind batter timing a cover drive by sound, a deaf captain signalling to his side, an LD player lifting a trophy, a PD bowler charging in at 80mph, or a child using a wheelchair competing at Lord's through Table Cricket, all embody the same truth:

PART THREE

CHAPTER TWENTY-FIVE: THE HISTORY AND EVOLUTION OF THE LAWS OF CRICKET

Early Informal Rules

- **16th–17th centuries**: When cricket was first played in villages in Kent and Sussex, there were no written rules, just local customs. Each village or club often had its own variations (how wide a bat could be, what counted as "out," etc.).

- Games were often linked to gambling, so disputes over rules were common. This drove the need for standardisation.

The First Written Laws (1744)

- In 1744, the first known written Laws of Cricket were drawn up by a group of London clubs, including members who played at the Artillery Ground in Finsbury.

- **These rules included:**

. Pitch length fixed at 22 yards.

. The stumps set 22 inches high, with a single bail.

. Bowlers had to deliver the ball underarm.

. Runs were recorded by "notches" cut on a stick with a knife (hence "scoring a notch").

The Marylebone Cricket Club (MCC) Takes Charge (1787)

- In 1787, the Marylebone Cricket Club (MCC) was founded at Lord's in London.

- The MCC became the custodian of the Laws and remains so today.

- From this point, all official changes went through MCC committees.

Key Changes Through the Centuries

- **1774** – LBW (Leg Before Wicket) rule introduced.

- **1835** – Round-arm bowling legalised.

- **1835** – Three stumps become standard (previously two).

- **1835** - The size of the bat fixed at a maximum width of 4.25 inches (thanks to a player turning up with a bat almost as wide as the stumps!).

- **1864** – Overarm bowling legalised.

- **1889-20th century** – Refinements on fielding restrictions, follow-on rules, no-ball and wide laws.

- **1960s** – Rise of protective gear and limited overs.

- **2000** – MCC undertakes a full rewrite, modernising language and clarifying terms.

- **2017** – Current version of the Laws (8th edition) introduced, including limits on bat thickness, updated rules on player conduct, and gender-neutral wording.

Today: Who Makes and Maintains the Laws?

- The MCC (Marylebone Cricket Club) still writes and maintains the Laws of Cricket.

- However, the International Cricket Council (ICC) governs the playing conditions for international matches (e.g. World Cups, Test series), meaning they can adapt the Laws for specific formats (ODIs, T20s).

- Domestic boards (like the England and Wales Cricket Board, ECB) use the MCC Laws as the foundation but may add regulations for competitions like The Hundred or T20 Blast.

Summary

- **1744**: First written Laws by London clubs.

- **1787**: MCC takes control as custodian of the Laws.

- **19th–20th centuries**: Major changes like overarm bowling, three stumps, and protective gear.

- **Today**: MCC maintains the Laws; ICC and national boards apply them to modern competitions.

CHAPTER TWENTY-SIX: THE HISTORY OF SCORING

Early Days: "Notches" on a Stick

- In the 16th and 17th centuries, when cricket was still a rustic village game, there were no official scorers.

- Runs were tallied using "notches" cut into a stick with a knife. Each run was a notch, hence the phrase "scoring a run."

- The sticks were sometimes carried by umpires or designated scorers, who cut marks as players ran between the wickets.

18th Century: Written Scorecards Appear

- By the 1740s, when the first Laws of Cricket were codified, scoring needed more precision, especially with the rise of gambling on matches.

- The first known printed scorecard appeared in 1776 for a match at Sevenoaks, Kent.

- These early scorecards were very basic: they listed the players' names, their runs, and who dismissed them. Bowling analyses were not yet recorded.

19th Century: The Age of Scorebooks and Symbols

- Scorebooks became common as cricket spread across England. Clubs developed their own recording systems.

- A scoring system of symbols was standardised:

. "b." for bowled, "c." for caught, "lbw" for leg before wicket.

. Extras (byes, leg byes, wides, no-balls) were added as separate categories.

- The box-style scorecard (batting order on one side, bowling analysis opposite) became the standard and is still used today.

- By the late 1800s, scorecards were being printed for spectators at major matches, helping cricket become more of a spectator sport.

The Role of the Official Scorer

- From the 19th century onwards, matches were usually recorded by two official scorers, one for each side.

- Each scorer sat together and cross-checked every ball with the umpire's signals. This practice continues in professional cricket today.

The Advent of Technology

- **20th Century**: Mechanical scoreboards became popular, showing runs, wickets, overs, and individual batsmen's scores to the crowd. Some iconic grounds, like Lord's and Headingley, still retain historic manual scoreboards alongside modern electronic ones.

- **Television era (1960s onwards)**: Live TV coverage meant detailed scoring needed to be fed to broadcasters. The teleprinter and early computers were used to relay scores quickly.

- **Digital revolution (1990s onwards)**: Scoring moved onto computerised systems, using software like TCS (Total Cricket Scorer). Ball-by-ball data could now be recorded instantly.

Today:

. Professional scorers use digital scoring apps linked to giant LED scoreboards.

. Fans can follow live ball-by-ball scoring on websites and apps worldwide.

. Analytics software tracks not just runs and wickets, but wagon wheels, strike rates, pitch maps, and advanced metrics.

Evolution of the Format

1. **Notches on a stick** → Simple tallies of runs.

2. **Early scorecards (1770s)** → Player names, runs, dismissals.

3. **19th century standardisation** → Batting/bowling columns, extras, partnerships.

4. **Mechanical scoreboards (20th c.)** → Scores displayed to crowds in real time.

5. **Electronic & digital systems (21st c.)** → Apps, live feeds, analytics, broadcast graphics.

CHAPTER TWENTY-SEVEN: THE HISTORY OF THE CRICKET BAT

Origins – The 16th & 17th Centuries

- The earliest reference to a cricket bat comes from 1624, when Jasper Vinall was killed after being struck by a fielder's bat-like implement.

- The first bats looked more like hockey sticks than modern bats: long, curved, and designed to hit a ball that was rolled along the ground (underarm bowling was the style then).

- These early bats were carved from a single piece of willow wood.

18th Century – The Straight Bat Emerges

- Around 1740s–1770s, bowlers began pitching the ball (bouncing it on the pitch rather than rolling).

- To counter this, batters needed a new shape → the straight bat appeared.

- By 1771, an infamous incident occurred when Thomas White used a bat as wide as the stumps to block everything, leading to the Law fixing the maximum width at 4.25 inches (10.8 cm), still the standard today.

19th Century – Refinement and Specialisation

Bats were now recognisably similar to modern versions:

. **Flat face** to control bounce.

. **Cane handles** are generally dated to the 1820s–1830s, but some historians argue the design was gradually adopted from the 1830s onward rather than instantly widespread.

. The **Splice** (a V-shaped joint where handle meets blade) was developed, improving durability.

- The "swell" (thick part of the blade) was introduced, giving more power.
- Famous bat makers like Gray-Nicolls and Gunn & Moore began producing bats commercially.

20th Century – From Utility to Science

- Early 1900s: Heavy, full-bodied bats suited to long, defensive innings.
- 1960s–70s: Limited-overs cricket encouraged lighter, more aggressive bats with thicker edges.
- 1979: The "aluminium bat incident" Australian Dennis Lillee used a metal bat in a Test, leading to a law requiring bats to be made of wood only.
- By the 1980s, bats were mass-manufactured with precision, balancing weight, pick-up, and power.

21st Century – Power Bats and Regulation

- Modern bats are thicker, with huge edges and deep swells, designed for T20 power hitting.
- New pressing techniques make the sweet spot bigger without adding much weight.

Controversy grew about bats giving batters too much advantage, so in 2017 the MCC changed the Laws:

. Max edge thickness = 40mm

. Max spine height = 67mm

. Bat width still capped at 4.25 inches

These changes tried to restore balance between bat and ball.

Materials and Craft

Willow is still the heart of the bat:

. English Willow: Softer, gives better performance, preferred at elite level.

. Kashmir Willow: Harder, cheaper, used in mass-market bats.

- Handles are reinforced with cane, rubber, and sometimes carbon fibre inserts for shock absorption.
- Grips and stickers add modern branding flair.

Famous Bats & Players

- **W.G. Grace** (19th c.) W. G. Grace used a heavy, long-bladed bat (with a relatively short handle), giving him immense reach
- **Don Bradman's "Don Bradman Special"** (1930s) became iconic.
- **Sachin Tendulkar** preferred a heavier bat (around 3lb 2oz), showing immense skill.
- **Chris Gayle** and modern T20 stars use thick-edged, power bats designed for six-hitting.

Today

- Bats are precision-engineered, a mix of traditional willow craftsmanship and modern design science.

- T20 cricket has pushed bat design towards lighter pick-up but explosive power, making six-hitting easier.

- Even smart bats are being tested, with sensors in the handle to measure bat speed, angles, and impact forces.

In short:

- **1600s:** Curved like hockey sticks.

- **1700s:** Straight bat emerges with pitched bowling.

- **1800s:** Splice, cane handles, power swell.

- **1900s:** Defensive to aggressive evolution, metal bat banned.

- **2000s+:** T20 "power bats," capped by MCC regulations.

- **Today:** Tradition meets tech, still willow but engineered for maximum performance.

CHAPTER TWENTY-EIGHT: THE HISTORY OF WICKETS

16th–17th Century: The Earliest Wickets

- In cricket's village origins, wickets were often just a tree stump, a gate, or a stick.

- The term "wicket" originally referred to a small gate in a fence (from Old English *wiket*). Early batsmen may literally have defended such gates!

- By the 1600s, wickets were usually made of two stumps in the ground, with a single crosspiece (bail) balanced across the top.

1744: First Written Laws

The earliest Laws of Cricket (1744) formalised the wicket:

. Two stumps only, 22 inches high and 6 inches wide.

. One bail laid across the top.

- This worked fine until bowlers began to pitch the ball and find gaps between the stumps.

Mid to late 1770s: The "Three Stump" Revolution

- In a famous match, bowler Lumpy Stevens bowled three deliveries clean through the gap between the stumps and the batter was not out because he hadn't hit wood!

- This caused outrage, and by 1774, the Laws were updated to add a third stump, closing the gap.

- The wicket was now 22 inches high and 6 inches wide, with two bails.

19th Century: Standardisation

- In 1814, the height of the stumps was raised to 24 inches, width increased to 7 inches.

- In 1835, the height was further raised to 27 inches, and the width fixed at 8 inches.

In 1865, the final modern dimensions were set:

. 28 inches high

. 9 inches wide

This remains the law today.

The Bails

- The bails have always been a quirky part of the wicket, two small wooden pieces, designed to fall when hit.

- The Laws specify that bails must be 4.31 inches long, with spigots that sit into grooves on the stumps.

- If bails cannot be used (usually due to wind), play continues. A batter can still be bowled or run out, but only if the umpire is satisfied the ball or fielder's action would have dislodged the bails if they had been in place

Materials and Design

- Traditionally made of ash or other hardwoods, both stumps and bails were hand-turned on a lathe.

- Today, stumps are still wood at professional level but may be reinforced for durability.

- Since the 1990s, high-profile matches use LED stumps and bails that light up when dislodged (branded "Zing" stumps).

Symbolism of the Wicket

The wicket has always been central to cricket's language:

. "Taking a wicket" = dismissing a batter.

. "Wickets in hand" = batting resources left.

. "The wicket" = the pitch itself.

. It's both a target and a metaphor for the game's strategy.

Fun Facts

- The world's oldest surviving set of stumps (1770s) is held at the MCC Museum at Lord's.
- In junior cricket, smaller wicket sizes are used to match pitch lengths.
- LED stumps can cost over £25,000 a set, compared to £30 for wooden ones!

In short:

- **1600s** – Tree stumps or gates.
- **1744** – Two stumps, one bail (22 inches high).
- **1775** – Third stump added after Lumpy Stevens incident.
- **19th c.** – Gradual increase in size.
- **1865** – Modern dimensions set: 28" x 9".
- **Today** – Still wooden at heart, but with LED technology for modern spectacle.

CHAPTER TWENTY-NINE: THE HISTORY OF THE CRICKET BALL

Origins – The Early Days (16th–17th Century)

- Cricket began in rural England, and the earliest balls were probably stones or tightly bound lumps of wool, rags, or cork, wrapped in leather.

- There was no standard size or weight; village matches often used whatever was available.

18th Century – Standardisation Begins

- By the early 1700s, cricket was becoming a gentleman's sport, and the need for standardised equipment grew.

- In 1774, the Laws of Cricket specified that a ball must weigh between 5.5 and 5.75 ounces and measure between approximately 8.7 and 9 inches in circumference, remarkably similar to today's.

- Balls were hand-stitched in four pieces of leather, forming the familiar "quarters," with a raised seam.

19th Century – The Rise of Dukes & Other Makers

- Duke & Son (founded in 1760 in London) perfected the art of the hand-stitched ball, which became the standard in England.

- The six-row seam design, with prominent stitching, allowed bowlers to generate swing and seam movement.

- By the late 1800s, cricket balls were being mass-produced but still required skilled hand-stitching.

20th Century – Evolution & Colour Variations

- Red balls dominated the sport, used in Tests and first-class cricket. They swing early in an innings and change character as they wear.

- White balls began experimental use in the late 1960s and became standard for day-night one-day cricket from the late 1970s.

- Pink balls arrived in the 2000s, designed for day-night Test cricket, easier to see in twilight but still with red-ball-like durability.

Ball Manufacturing – How It's Made

1. **Core**: Layers of tightly wound cork and twine form the hard inner core.

2. **Leather Cover**: Four pieces of high-quality leather are cut, dyed (red, white, or pink), and shaped.

3. **Stitching**: The leather pieces are hand-stitched with strong linen thread; six rows form the seam.

4. **Polishing**: Balls are lacquered and polished to enhance durability and swing.

Key Modern Makers

- **Dukes (England)** – Famous for producing balls that swing late and heavily.

- **Kookaburra (Australia)** – Used in most international matches outside England; has a less pronounced seam and loses swing earlier.

- **SG (Sanspareils Greenlands, India)** – Used in Indian Test matches; softer seam, offering more grip for spinners.

Today's Innovations

- According to MCC Law 4 (also used in ICC playing conditions), cricket balls must weigh 155.9–163 g for men and 140–151 g for women, with a circumference of 22.4–22.9 cm for men and 21.0–22.5 cm for women.

- Smart ball technology is being trialled, with microchips inside to track speed, spin, seam position, and swing, turning the ball into a data source.

- Discussions continue on how to balance balls for bat-dominant formats like T20, where white balls don't swing much.

Fun Facts

- The oldest surviving cricket ball (early 1700s) is preserved at the MCC Museum, made of leather with a cork core.

- In 2007, the first pink balls were tested in domestic cricket before being used in day-night Tests from 2015.

- The durability of balls is such a factor that teams choose suppliers strategically; e.g., England favouring Dukes in home Tests for extra swing.

PART FOUR

CHAPTER THIRTY: GROUND STAFF.

THE HIDDEN FORCE IN CRICKET.

Cricket is made possible, prepared, maintained, and rescued time and again by a group whose names are rarely known: the ground staff. From the hum of an old roller at a village club to the whirr of high-tech mowers at Lord's, their work underpins every run, wicket, and cheer the game produces.

Grassroots Heroes

At local clubs, the ground staff are often volunteers. They are coaches, parents, or retired players who rise early on Saturday mornings to mow the square, roll the wicket, and mark the creases with chalked lines that vanish by tea. Their equipment is often held together with ingenuity, a roller built decades ago, a mower that requires more coaxing than cutting, or a line-marker improvised from a pram wheel. Yet these unsung caretakers are the heartbeat of village cricket.

Former England captain Michael Vaughan has often spoken of the volunteers at Sheffield Collegiate CC, saying:

"We thought our coaches were the heroes, but really it was the old boys on the roller at 7am making sure we had somewhere to play. Without them, none of us would have had a game."

At women's clubs across the country, that dedication has been no different. At Wantage Road, Northampton, members of the women's section recall their own parents marking out pitches by hand in the 1990s, long before the women's game had professional grounds staff support.

The Big Stage: County and Test Grounds

Step up to the county grounds and Test arenas, and the scale changes, but the philosophy remains the same. Here, ground staff are professionals whose knowledge borders on scientific. They read soil, moisture and weather with the precision of meteorologists. They prepare pitches weeks in advance, balancing grass cover, moisture content, and hardness to ensure contests are fair but lively.

At places like Headingley, Edgbaston, or The Oval, the ground staff become part of the match narrative, their sprint with the covers in a summer downpour as dramatic as any boundary or wicket.

Australian legend Shane Warne once admitted:

"In England, you never play just against the eleven on the field, you're playing the groundsmen too. They know how to make a pitch sing or stay quiet. The good ones are real artists."

At Chelmsford, home of Essex and the England Women's team for many summers, the ground staff became integral to the rise of women's international cricket. Players like Charlotte Edwards often spoke of their gratitude to the crew who ensured the surface at Chelmsford was always fast, fair, and crowd-ready, making it one of the best-loved venues in the women's game.

Drama in the Rain

One of the most iconic sights in English cricket is the coordinated charge of the ground staff as rain sweeps in. Spectators groan, players rush for the dressing room, but for the staff, this is the moment. With military precision, they unroll huge sheets of plastic to protect the square, wrestling against wind and rain.

Umpire Dickie Bird recalled a near-disaster at Headingley in the 1980s:

"The rain came like a wall, and within minutes the outfield was a lake. I thought we'd be abandoned for sure. But the lads came flying out, sliding about in the mud, and somehow saved the pitch. By tea we were back on. People forget, they saved that match, not me."

In 2017 at Taunton, when England Women faced South Africa in a World Cup clash, a sudden summer downpour threatened to derail play. The ground staff worked through sheets of rain with super-soppers and blowers, allowing the game to restart. England won, and the staff received a round of applause from players and fans alike.

Legendary Figures

Some groundsmen have become legends in their own right. At Lord's, Mick Hunt, head groundsman for over 40 years, was revered for his ability to produce pitches that balanced bat and ball with artistry. At Headingley, Andy Fogarty has overseen countless dramatic Tests, including the famous 2019 Ashes miracle when Ben Stokes' heroics would not have been possible without a perfectly prepared surface.

Ben Stokes acknowledged their unseen role:

"Everyone remembers the sixes and the crowd, but I'll never forget that pitch. It gave us a chance, and that's down to the ground staff. They gave me the stage to perform on."

In the women's game, the move to professionalism has highlighted new trailblazers. At Hove, where Sussex Women played much of their cricket, the grounds staff under Andy Mackay developed hybrid pitches and worked alongside England's women to provide surfaces worthy of global tournaments.

Unsung Sacrifices

The life of groundsmen, and increasingly, groundswomen, is relentless. Matches finish late, and they may be out at dawn again the next day, rolling, cutting, or patching scars on the pitch. In winter, they battle frost, cover squares, and protect outfields from the elements. Their work is unglamorous and often unnoticed until something goes wrong.

Former umpire Simon Taufel once put it best:

"If the umpires are invisible when we do our job, the ground staff are ghosts. But they're the ones who make sure there's actually a game to umpire."

In women's domestic cricket, many county grounds still rely on mixed crews of staff and volunteers. At Yorkshire Diamonds, one long-time volunteer recalled painting boundaries in the morning before heading off to sell tickets and man the scoreboard. The sense of pride was enormous: "It didn't matter if it was men's or women's, it was Yorkshire cricket, and we made it happen."

Why They Matter

Cricket is unique among sports in the degree to which its playing surface shapes the game. A football pitch is a canvas; a cricket pitch is a living, breathing character in the drama. Its bounce, pace, and turn can define the contest. That responsibility rests entirely with groundstaff. Their skill ensures fairness, safety, and spectacle.

The Hidden Force

In truth, cricket's greatest spectacles, Headingley 1981, Edgbaston 2005, Lord's finals, Chelmsford under lights, would not have been possible without the silent army of ground staff. From grassroots volunteers marking wickets with string, to professional crews saving a Test from torrential rain, they are the game's hidden force.

Or, as Alastair Cook once put it in his understated way:

"We win matches, but they make cricket possible."

Women on the Ground: Breaking New Turf

For generations, groundskeeping was seen as a man's world, heavy rollers, long days in the elements, and a role tucked away behind the scenes. But in recent years, women have begun to break into this space, proving that maintaining cricket's sacred turf is not defined by gender but by skill, knowledge, and passion.

- **Megan White (Australia)** – One of the first women to join the MCG ground staff, she became a familiar sight preparing the most famous strip in Australian cricket. White has spoken about the pride of seeing players walk onto a surface she prepared:

"You know the whole world is watching, but for us it's just about getting it right, grass length, moisture, bounce. It's precision, not gender."

- **Sarah Derrick (England)** – A pioneering figure at Somerset CCC, Derrick worked her way into the ground staff at Taunton. Her role during the 2017 Women's World Cup, ensuring pitches were ready for global TV audiences, was widely praised.

- **Claire Taylor (not the cricketer)** – One of the first women employed by a county in a permanent role in outfield maintenance. At Northamptonshire, she proved that attention to detail, resilience, and turf science matter more than tradition.

- **ECB Initiatives** – In 2021 the ECB launched a recruitment push to diversify ground staff, with female apprentices placed at county clubs. This has been mirrored in Australia and India, where women are now part of the maintenance crews at domestic and international venues.

- **Inspirational Volunteers** – Across England, women volunteers at grassroots level have long been quietly keeping clubs alive, painting boundary lines, setting up wickets, and tending squares for their children's matches.

Their contribution, often unrecognised, has been as vital as any professional groundsman's.

The presence of women on ground staff teams has changed perceptions in two ways:

1. **Representation** – Young girls now see women not just batting or bowling but preparing the pitches themselves.

2. **Professionalisation of Women's Cricket** – As women's international cricket has grown, so too has the demand for equal-quality surfaces. Female ground staff have often been at the forefront of ensuring parity.

As Charlotte Edwards once said after a World Cup warm-up:

"When I saw women out there preparing the pitch for us, I knew the game was changing. It felt like cricket was finally ours too, from grass to glory."

The Future of Ground Staff

As cricket faces the 21st century, so too does the work of its ground staff evolve.

- **Climate change** is reshaping their role. Hotter summers dry out pitches faster, while unpredictable storms make covers and drainage systems more vital than ever. Groundsmen and women are now weather watchers, adjusting preparation on the fly.

- **Technology** is revolutionising their toolkit. Hover covers glide across pitches at Lord's, drones monitor outfield moisture, and soil sensors measure data to an inch.

- **Hybrid pitches** – blends of natural turf and artificial fibres are being trialled to extend durability and balance bat-and-ball contests, particularly in multi-format venues that host men's and women's fixtures back-to-back.

- **Sustainability** is becoming central: many counties are reducing water use, recycling rainwater, and switching to electric rollers and mowers.

Future generations of fans may never notice these changes, and that's the point. The best ground staff make the extraordinary look ordinary. As conditions grow tougher, their skill, adaptability, and quiet dedication will be more important than ever.

CHAPTER THIRTY-ONE: THE BARMY ARMY

From Beer-Soaked Beginnings to Global Force

If Test cricket is sometimes accused of being too quiet, too stately, and too much like a genteel afternoon in a members' pavilion, then the Barmy Army is living proof that the stereotype doesn't always hold.

They are loud. They are passionate. They are relentlessly inventive with song and chant. And from their accidental beginnings on an England tour in the mid-1990s, they have become one of the most recognisable supporter groups in world sport.

Origins: Ashes, Adelaide, and a Few Too Many Beers

The story of the Barmy Army begins in the 1994-95 Ashes tour of Australia. England, led by Mike Atherton, were a side in transition and, truth be told, not expected to do much against Allan Border's Australians. What England *did* have, however, was a small band of die-hard supporters who had travelled across the world to follow their team, regardless of results.

At the Adelaide Test, a group of England fans, fuelled by equal parts beer and blind optimism, began singing their hearts out even as England were being thrashed. The Australian press, half amused, and half exasperated, dubbed them the "Barmy Army."

The name stuck.

These fans, many of them young and travelling, had found a way of turning misery on the pitch into joy in the stands. Instead of sulking about yet another batting collapse, they sang football-style terrace chants, waved St George's flags, and turned Test cricket into a carnival.

Growing Pains: From Pub to Organisation

Through the late 1990s, the Barmy Army grew from an informal group of travellers into a more organised force. Founders like Paul Burnham and Dave Peacock began selling shirts and songbooks, organising tickets, and giving the movement a bit of structure.

At first, county cricket purists and MCC traditionalists weren't entirely sure what to make of them. Lords' wasn't built for brass bands and terrace chants. But the Army kept growing, and players themselves soon admitted that hearing "Jerusalem" bellowed from the stands gave them a lift.

The Barmy Army's most famous chants weren't sophisticated; they were catchy, repetitive, and often cheekily targeted at opposition players. Shane Warne, Ricky Ponting, and Glenn McGrath were all serenaded over the years. Even umpires and grounds staff weren't immune to a bit of Barmy ribbing.

Expansion: Beyond the Ashes

By the 2000s, the Barmy Army had become an institution. Thousands of fans now joined them on every Ashes tour, often out-singing and out-numbering home support. Their sea of red and white flags became a fixture in grounds from Perth to Sydney.

But the Army didn't stop at Australia. They turned up in South Africa, the Caribbean, India, Sri Lanka, New Zealand, Pakistan, and beyond. Wherever England played, the Barmy Army followed, often forming the loudest section of the crowd.

They also built relationships with local communities. In Sri Lanka and India, Barmy supporters often shared stands with local fans, swapping songs and drinks. In the Caribbean, their trumpeters and drummers turned Tests into parties that rivalled the West Indian steel drums.

Songs, Trumpets, and the Famous Faces

A Barmy Army matchday is a spectacle in itself. There's always a trumpeter, most famously Billy Cooper, nicknamed "Billy the Trumpet," who played everything from "The Great Escape" to the theme tune from *Neighbours* in Australian grounds.

Songs are simple, humorous, and relentless. They recycle football terrace standards, "Stand Up if You Love England" and invent their own classics.

Players themselves have often joined in. Andrew Flintoff and Kevin Pietersen were both serenaded with Barmy chants. Even opposition players sometimes admitted enjoying it, Merv Hughes once said, "You know you've made it when the Barmy Army sing a song about you."

The Professional Era: Charity, Merch, and Organisation

As their numbers swelled, the Barmy Army professionalised. They became an official supporters' club, with a website, memberships, merchandise, and organised tours. They weren't just a drunken rabble; they were a global fan movement.

The Army also embraced charity work. Over the years, they have raised thousands for good causes, often in the host countries they visit. Schools in Sri Lanka, children's charities in Australia, and community projects in the Caribbean have all benefited from Barmy donations.

This gave them credibility beyond just noise in the stands. They became ambassadors for English cricket abroad, even when the team was struggling.

Criticism and Controversy

Not everyone loved the Barmy Army. Some traditionalists argued they were too loud, too boisterous, and not in keeping with the spirit of Test cricket. Australian newspapers sometimes painted them as drunken nuisances. Even the England & Wales Cricket Board (ECB) had moments of nervousness about their antics.

But the criticism rarely stuck. The truth was that the Barmy Army were filling grounds, creating atmosphere, and keeping Test cricket relevant for a younger audience. As one journalist wrote: "Without the Barmy Army, some England away Tests would sound like funerals."

How Big Are They Now?

Today, the Barmy Army is a global brand. Membership runs into the tens of thousands, and on Ashes tours their numbers can reach 30,000-40,000 across the series. Their website sells merchandise worldwide, their official travel arm arranges packages, and their trumpeters are minor celebrities.

They are also an export model: other nations now have their own supporter groups, the Australian "Fanatics," India's Bharat Army, Pakistan's Stani Army, but the Barmy Army remain the originals, and the loudest.

More Than Just Noise

At its heart, the Barmy Army are about joy. They are about following a team through thick and thin, about refusing to sit in silence when the batting collapses again and about finding humour in heartbreak.

For players, the Army has become a constant. Win or lose, home or away, there is always a red-and-white sea singing for England.

As Nasser Hussain once said:

"You know you're never alone when the Barmy Army are in the ground. They'll back you whatever the scoreline."

CONCLUSION

From a few young lads in Adelaide to a global phenomenon, the Barmy Army have rewritten what it means to be a Test cricket fan. They are part brass band, part football terrace, part travelling circus and wholly English.

And while England's fortunes rise and fall, one thing remains constant: somewhere in the stands, trumpet blaring, songs echoing, pints flowing, and flags waving, the Barmy Army will be there.

Top 5 Barmy Army Chants

The Barmy Army don't do subtle, their songs are catchy, repetitive, and guaranteed to get stuck in your head for days. Here are five of their all-time favourites:

1. "The Great Escape" (Trumpet Theme)

. Billy the Trumpet's signature tune. Every time he blares it out, the crowd takes over with claps and shouts. Even opposition fans join in.

2. "We Are the Army, the Barmy Army"

. Sung to the tune of *The Animals Went in Two by Two*.

> . A rolling anthem of loyalty (and mild madness):
> *"We are the Army, the Barmy Army,
> And we are mental, and we are mad…"*

3. **"Stand Up If You Love England"**

. Simple but effective. A ripple starts in one corner of the ground and soon thousands are on their feet, arms raised, roaring it out.

4. **"You All Live in a Shane Warne House"**

. A cheeky reworking of *Yellow Submarine*, sung endlessly at the great Australian spinner. Part admiration, part wind-up. Warne himself later admitted he found it funny (eventually).

5. **"Everywhere We Go"**

A classic football terrace chant adapted for cricket:

> *"Everywhere we go… people want to know…*
> *Who we are… where we come from…*
> *And we tell them… we are England…*
> *The Barmy Barmy England!"*

Top 5 Player-Specific Barmy Army Chants

1. **Ricky Ponting – "Four More Years"**

. After Australia's 2005 Ashes defeat, Ponting vowed they'd come back stronger. The Barmy Army pounced, serenading him with *"Four more years, four more years…"* every time he came out to bat. He admitted later it drove him nuts.

2. **Mitchell Johnson – "He Bowls to the Left…"**

Sung to the tune of *Knees Up Mother Brown*:

> *"He bowls to the left,*
> *He bowls to the right,*
> *That Mitchell Johnson,*
> *His bowling is sh**e!"*

Brutal but unforgettable. Johnson later said it got into his head during the 2009 Ashes.

3. **Shane Warne – "He Eats All the Pies"**

To the tune of *Knees Up Mother Brown* again:

> *"You're fat, you're round,*
> *Your ar*e is on the ground,*
> *Shane Warne, Shane Warne…"*

Warne, being Warne, usually gave a cheeky grin back to the crowd.

4. **David Warner – "You've Got Small Hands"**

Borrowed from football chants, England fans latched onto Warner with a chorus of *"You've got small hands"* sung repeatedly while he fielded near the boundary. Petty, funny, and impossible to ignore.

5. **Glenn McGrath – "You'll Never Get a 5-For"**

Whenever McGrath had four wickets, the Barmy Army would belt this out until either he broke through… or he didn't. The mixture of pressure and banter gave it legendary status.

CHAPTER THIRTY-TWO: RED BALL V WHITE BALL V PINK BALL IN CRICKET

Have you ever wondered why some games are referred to 'a Red Ball match' and others white? Well, wonder no more.

1. The Ball Itself

- **Red Ball**

. Used in Test matches and first-class cricket.

. Made with traditional red dye and a harder, more durable seam.

. Lasts longer (can be used for up to 80 overs before replacement).

. Ages and deteriorates in a way that produces swing (especially early) and reverse swing (later).

- **White Ball**

. Used in limited-overs cricket (One-Day Internationals and T20s).

. Coated with a protective lacquer to keep it visible under floodlights.

. Tends to stay bright for only 25–30 overs, so ODIs often use two balls (one from each end) to last the innings.

. Swings less for bowlers, making it more batter-friendly.

2. Match Formats

- **Red Ball** → Long format cricket (Tests, 4-day county matches).
- **White Ball** → Short format cricket (ODIs, T20s, The Hundred).

3. Playing Conditions

- **Red Ball Cricket**

. Played in the daytime.

. Red ball easier to see against white clothing and natural light.

. Games last 4-5 days, so conditions change over time (pitch wears, ball ages).

- **White Ball Cricket**

. Often played under lights (day-night games).

. White ball is easier to see under floodlights when players wear coloured kits.

. Matches limited to 20 or 50 overs per side, so designed for quicker results.

4. Style of Play

- **Red Ball**

. Tests patience, technique, and stamina.

. Bowlers rely on swing, seam, and spin over long spells.

. Batters aim to build long innings and wear down opponents.

- **White Ball**

. Faster, more aggressive style.

. Batters play attacking shots (power hitting, strike rotation).

. Bowlers use variations (Yorkers, slower balls, bouncers) to contain runs.

5. Strategy & Spectacle

- **Red Ball Cricket** = The "traditional" form. Considered the ultimate test of skill, endurance, and tactical depth.
- **White Ball Cricket** = The "entertainment" form. Designed for TV audiences, with coloured clothing, floodlights, and big hitting.

In short:

- Red ball = endurance, tradition, skill over time (Tests & first-class).

- White ball = entertainment, speed, attacking play (ODIs & T20s).

The Pink Ball in Cricket

The pink cricket ball was introduced as part of the game's evolution to make day–night Test matches possible. Traditional red balls, used in men's and women's Tests, tend to lose visibility under floodlights, while white balls, used in limited-overs cricket, can be difficult to see against players' white clothing in the longer format. The pink ball solved both problems. Its brighter colour gives better visibility under lights and allows the spectacle of Test cricket to be extended into the evening, helping attract larger crowds and television audiences.

The Pink Ball in Women's Cricket

In women's cricket, the pink ball has taken on a particular significance. Women's international teams now use it in day–night Tests and domestic competitions, giving them the chance to play in prime-time slots and showcase the longest format of the game to wider audiences. The ball behaves slightly differently to the traditional red, with its harder lacquer and seam meaning it can swing for longer but may not deteriorate in quite the same way. This has created fresh tactical challenges for captains and bowlers. More importantly, the pink ball has symbolised a step toward equality: by allowing women's matches to be staged under lights and broadcast to evening audiences, it places them on the same global stage as the men's game.

The Dimensions and Weight of the Pink Ball in the Women's Game

Although the colour of the ball is different, the dimensions and weight of the pink cricket ball in women's cricket follow the same Laws of Cricket that apply to all formats, with specific adjustments for the women's game. According to the Marylebone Cricket Club (MCC) Laws, which govern the sport worldwide:

· **Women's Test, ODI, and T20 cricket** use a slightly smaller and lighter ball than the men's game.

· The women's ball must weigh between 4.94 and 5.31 ounces (140–151 grams).

· Its circumference must be between 8 25/16 inches and 8 13/16 inches (21.0–22.4 cm).

By contrast, the men's ball weighs 155.9–163 grams and is slightly larger in circumference.

The pink ball used in women's cricket is manufactured to these specifications, but it also has an extra layer of shiny lacquer compared with the red ball. This helps preserve the colour under floodlights, prevents the ball from turning dull too quickly, and ensures it remains visible for both players and spectators throughout the evening sessions of day–night matches.

This size and weight difference has a subtle impact on play. Bowlers, especially seamers, can swing the lighter women's ball for longer periods, while spinners may find it grips slightly differently depending on the condition of the pitch. Batters, on the other hand, often comment that the pink ball can "skid on" more under lights, making timing both a challenge and an opportunity.

CHAPTER THIRTY-THREE: THE STORY OF THE TEST MATCH

The Story of Test Cricket

Test cricket is often described as the purest form of the game, a format where skill, stamina, patience, and nerve are tested over five long days. It is the game in its most traditional sense, but also the one that produces some of the most dramatic and emotional moments in cricketing history. To understand Test cricket is to understand the soul of the sport itself.

The Birth of Test Cricket

The story begins in March 1877, when England travelled by sea to face Australia at the Melbourne Cricket Ground. That match, retrospectively recognised as the first official Test, set the template for everything that followed. The Australians won by 45 runs, sending shockwaves through a cricketing world that had assumed England's superiority.

Five years later, in 1882, a famous satirical obituary in *The Sporting Times* marked "the death of English cricket" after Australia defeated England at The Oval. The "Ashes" were born, and with them the fiercest and most enduring rivalry in the sport.

"A Test match is like life itself, sometimes slow, sometimes thrilling, but always worth the journey." - **Richie Benaud**

Women Enter the Arena

While men's Test cricket dominated the early decades, women were quietly carving their own place in the sport. In December 1934, just over half a century after the first men's Test, the first women's Test match was played in Brisbane between England and Australia. England, captained by Betty Archdale, won the series 2–1, and so began the Women's Ashes.

Though resources and attention were often limited, pioneering women's cricketers showed extraordinary resilience. In 1935, the England women played their first Test on home soil at Northampton, and gradually, through the 1950s and 1960s, women's Test cricket established itself, though with fewer fixtures compared to the men's calendar.

"We didn't play for crowds or money. We played because we loved the game, and because we wanted to prove that women belonged on the cricket field too."
- **Rachael Heyhoe Flint**

Expansion and New Frontiers

Men's cricket expanded globally in the mid-20th century. India's 1932 debut at Lord's, Pakistan's arrival in 1952, and Sri Lanka's entry in 1982 reflected the game's spreading popularity. Famous series became part of national identities, the West Indies' dominance in the 1970s and 1980s, driven by their fearsome fast bowlers, set a new standard for Test excellence.

For women, the post-war years also saw growth. By the 1970s, more nations began fielding women's teams, including New Zealand and India. The first Indian women's Test came in 1976 against the West Indies, with **Diana Edulji** emerging as one of the game's great early ambassadors.

"Cricket is not defined by gender. A cover drive is a cover drive, whether it is played at Lord's or Eden Gardens, by a man or a woman." - **Diana Edulji**

Iconic Moments in Test History

Test cricket's legend has always been built on its ability to produce the extraordinary. For men, there have been countless classics:

· The Tied Test of 1960 between Australia and the West Indies in Brisbane, the first of its kind.

· England's 2005 Ashes victory, when Andrew Flintoff and Kevin Pietersen helped topple a mighty Australian side.

· Ben Stokes' miraculous innings at Headingley in 2019, when his unbeaten 135 dragged England to a one-wicket win.

For women, the heroics have been just as memorable:

· In 2005, the England women also reclaimed the Ashes after 42 years, led by Clare Connor.

· In 2014, India beat England at Wormsley, led by Mithali Raj and Jhulan Goswami, a watershed for Indian women's cricket.

· In 2023, Tammy Beaumont scored a record-breaking 208 against Australia at Trent Bridge.

"If you don't enjoy Test cricket, you don't enjoy cricket at all." - **Sunil Gavaskar**

"To score runs in a Test is the greatest satisfaction you can have as a cricketer." - **Tammy Beaumont**

The Test Match Experience

What makes a Test unique is not only the cricket itself, but the culture around it. Over five days, fans come and go, weather plays its part, sessions ebb and flow. A single delivery in the first hour of day one can ripple into decisive drama on day five.

Women's Test matches, usually played over four days and not five, though played less frequently, carry the same sense of occasion. When England women hosted

Australia at Trent Bridge in 2023, nearly 24,000 fans attended, and millions watched highlights worldwide. Every run and wicket mattered, reminding fans that the long format still has a vital place in the women's game.

"It tests you mentally, physically, emotionally, that's why it's called a Test." - **Virat Kohli**

"We don't just want to play cricket. We want to play the best cricket and that means Tests." - **Ellyse Perry**

Modern Challenges and the Future

By the 21st century, Test cricket faced new challenges. The rise of ODIs in the 1970s and T20 in the 2000s provided shorter, more marketable versions of the game. Yet, far from dying, the longest format has adapted. The World Test Championship, launched in 2019, gave global context and extra meaning to bilateral series.

For women, the campaign for more Tests continues. Players like Heather Knight and Smriti Mandhana have stressed the need for more opportunities in the longest format. Knight's century in the 2022 Ashes Test at Canberra, and Mandhana's fluent 127 in 2021 against Australia, both highlighted just how compelling women's Test cricket can be.

CONCLUSION: THE PINNACLE OF CRICKET

From the very first match in 1877 to the epic battles of today, Test cricket remains the ultimate examination of a cricketer's ability. For men and women alike, it is the stage where legends are made, where patience and courage are tested, and where the spirit of cricket shines brightest.

Whether it is Bradman at The Oval, Sobers in Kingston, Flintoff at Edgbaston, Perry at North Sydney, or Beaumont at Trent Bridge, the stories of Test cricket are etched deep into the game's fabric. Formats may come and go, but the red ball, the whites, and the five-day contest endure.

And in the stands, whether it is the Barmy Army belting out songs in Sydney, kids waving flags in Nottingham, or Caribbean crowds dancing to the sound of drums, the fans remain part of the story. Without them, Test cricket would be incomplete.

"People ask if Test cricket has a future. As long as it still makes you cry, cheer, and sit on the edge of your seat, it will always have a future." - **Mike Atherton**

CHAPTER THIRTY-FOUR: THE WORLD TEST CHAMPIONSHIP.

For more than a century, Test cricket has been considered the pinnacle of the sport. Five days of strategy, endurance, skill, and mental toughness make it the ultimate examination of a cricketer's ability. And yet, for most of its history, Test cricket lacked one crucial ingredient: a true global competition. Unlike football's World Cup or rugby's Six Nations, Test matches were always bilateral series, England v Australia in the Ashes, India v Pakistan in fierce rivalries, or West Indies v England in historic battles. These contests were passionate, yes, but they never led to a definitive answer to the biggest question of all: Who is the world's best Test team?

The ICC World Test Championship (WTC) was born to answer that question.

The Road to a Test Championship

As far back as the 1990s, cricket administrators floated the idea of a "Test league." But the logistics of fitting a proper tournament into the already jam-packed international calendar made it seem impossible. Instead, Test matches rolled on in cycles, sometimes meaningful, sometimes not.

The closest thing to a world champion in the 20th century was the unofficial ICC Test Rankings table, launched in 2003. Teams like Australia (under Steve Waugh and Ricky Ponting), South Africa, and India took turns at the top, but fans often dismissed rankings as abstract mathematics. What supporters wanted was a *final*, a trophy, and bragging rights.

Finally, in 2019, after years of planning, the International Cricket Council (ICC) launched the World Test Championship. The goal was simple: add context and a global climax to the oldest form of the game.

How It Works

The WTC runs in two-year cycles. Each Test-playing nation plays a set number of series (home and away) against different opponents. Unlike the County

Championship or a football league, not every team plays every other team, but each has the chance to earn points.

- **Points system:** Teams earn points for wins and draws (the exact structure has evolved, but every Test in the cycle counts).
- **League table:** At the end of the cycle, the top two teams qualify for a Final.
- **The Final:** Played over five days at a neutral ground (so far always in England), this single match crowns the official World Test Champions.

It was a radical idea: after 140 years of bilateral Tests, cricket now had a global Test tournament.

The First World Test Championship Final (2019–21)

The inaugural WTC cycle ran from August 2019 to June 2021. It was disrupted badly by COVID-19, with several tours postponed or cancelled. But despite the chaos, two teams rose above the rest: India and New Zealand.

- **Venue: Southampton, England (Ageas Bowl).**
- **Conditions:** Rain washed out large parts of the game, turning it into a tense, stop-start affair.
- **Result:** New Zealand triumphed by 8 wickets, chasing down a modest target with captain Kane Williamson and Ross Taylor guiding them home.

It was a historic moment. New Zealand, long regarded as underdogs in world cricket, had finally won a global ICC trophy. For India, it was another heartbreak, adding to their list of near misses in major finals.

The Second Cycle (2021–23)

The next two-year cycle built even more interest. England, South Africa, Sri Lanka, Pakistan, and West Indies all fought hard, but once again, two giants emerged: India and Australia.

- **Venue:** The Oval, London.
- **The Story:** Australia's batting and relentless pace attack proved too much for India. Steve Smith and Travis Head piled on runs, while Pat Cummins, Scott Boland, and Mitchell Starc dismantled India's batting line-up.
- **Result:** Australia won comfortably, lifting the WTC mace for the first time.

For Australia, it was the ultimate confirmation of their Test dominance - Ashes winners, and now the official world champions. For India, it was déjà vu: two finals, two defeats.

Why It Matters

The World Test Championship has done more than hand out trophies. It has:

- **Given context:** Every Test series now carries weight beyond local rivalries. A West Indies–Sri Lanka match might once have been overlooked, but in the WTC era, it could shape the table.
- **Boosted fan interest:** The idea of a "league table" appeals to younger fans used to T20 leagues and tournaments.
- **Crowned champions:** At last, Test cricket has a single, undisputed champion at the end of each cycle.

The Future of the WTC:

As the competition grows for the men's game, several questions remain:

- **Venues:** Should finals continue in England, or rotate across Test nations like Australia, India, or South Africa?
- **Format:** Some argue for semi-finals to give more teams a shot at the final.
- **Balance:** With so much attention on T20 leagues like the IPL, the WTC provides a crucial anchor to keep Test cricket alive and relevant.

But what is clear is this: the WTC has already added prestige to Test cricket. When New Zealand lifted the trophy in 2021, and when Australia followed in 2023, it felt like history being made.

The Missing Piece – A Women's World Test Championship?

While the men's World Test Championship has quickly become an established feature of international cricket, there remains a glaring gap: there is no women's equivalent.

Women's Test cricket has a proud history stretching back to 1934, when England and Australia played the very first women's Test at Brisbane. Over the decades, Test matches became the most prestigious format for female cricketers, with iconic contests like the Women's Ashes producing legends. Yet, unlike the men's game, women's Tests have always been played far less frequently.

Why Isn't There a Women's WTC?

There are a few reasons:

- **Scheduling:** Most women's international tours are focused on limited-overs cricket, particularly ODIs and T20s, which link to the World Cup and the Olympic future of T20.

- **Commercial pull:** Broadcasters and sponsors have been quicker to back white-ball formats, which provide faster matches and higher viewing figures.

- **Logistics:** With fewer women's Test matches on the calendar, it's difficult to create a fair league system like the men's WTC.

But the appetite is growing. Players regularly call for more Test matches, and fans point out that some of the greatest moments in women's cricket, such as England v Australia's thrilling draws in the Women's Ashes, come in the longest format.

Looking Ahead

If the ICC and national boards can balance the international calendar, a Women's World Test Championship could easily become the next big milestone in the global game. Just as the women's T20 World Cup has grown into a major sporting event, a WTC would give structure, purpose, and glory to the red-ball format in the women's game.

And when that day comes, the sight of a women's team lifting the Test mace will be a landmark moment, a declaration that Test cricket, the crown jewel of the sport, shines equally for men and women.

Test Cricket's Crown

Test cricket will always be about tradition, rivalries, and timeless battles. The Ashes, India v Pakistan, and South Africa v Australia need no extra incentive. But the World Test Championship has added something Test cricket never had before: a crowning moment.

From Kane Williamson lifting the trophy in the rain at Southampton to Pat Cummins holding it high at The Oval, the WTC has ensured that the longest format of the game now has its rightful crown.

The mace, once given only to the No.1 ranked team, now belongs to the champions of the Test world.

At last, the question has an answer: **Who is the best Test team on earth?**

CHAPTER THIRTY-FIVE: THE TWENTY20

A Bold Experiment

The year was 2003. English county cricket faced a problem: dwindling crowds, shrinking sponsorship, and the sense that Test matches and one-day games weren't enough to attract a younger audience. The England and Wales Cricket Board (ECB) decided to try something daring, a brand-new format called Twenty20 cricket, in which each side faced just 20 overs.

The idea was simple: a match that could be completed in about three hours, perfect for an evening out. Less time-consuming than a one-day international, far more explosive than a County Championship game. Floodlights, coloured kits, pop music, and a family-friendly ticket price. Cricket repackaged as a short, sharp spectacle.

On 13 June 2003, the first official Twenty20 match was played between the English counties. Fans turned up in fancy dress, beer snakes climbed the stands, and the players themselves sensed this was something new. It was cricket, but with the shackles off.

The Rules That Changed the Game

T20 didn't just shorten the overs. It rewrote the feel of cricket:

- **20 overs per side**; matches last about 3 hours.

- **Fielding restrictions** to encourage attacking shots.

- **Batters free to innovate**: the reverse-sweep, the ramp, the switch-hit became mainstream.

- **Crowd-friendly extras**: DJs, fireworks, music between overs.

Where Test cricket was chess and ODIs were checkers, T20 felt like an arcade game, fast, colourful, unpredictable.

The Global Explosion

Other nations quickly took note. By 2005, T20 internationals had begun. The first men's T20 World Cup was held in South Africa in 2007, a tournament remembered for Yuvraj Singh's six sixes in an over and India's dramatic victory over Pakistan in the final.

This was a watershed moment. India, cricket's financial giant, suddenly had the perfect product to market. By 2008, the Indian Premier League (IPL) was born. It combined Bollywood glitz, corporate money, and the world's best players into a franchise system. Cricket had never seen anything like it. Packed stadiums, cheerleaders, player auctions, and astronomical TV rights deals turned the IPL into the richest cricket league on the planet.

Other leagues soon followed:

- **Big Bash League (Australia)** – carnival atmosphere, family-first marketing.

- **Pakistan Super League (PSL)** – a showcase of Pakistan's batting flair and fast bowling.

- **Caribbean Premier League (CPL)** – cricket played like a street festival, complete with drums and dancing.

- **Bangladesh Premier League (BPL), SA20 (South Africa), ILT20 (UAE)** each carving its niche.

T20 had gone global.

The English Relationship

Ironically, while England invented T20, it was slow to embrace it at the highest level. The early years of the T20 World Cup saw England underperform, even as Indian, West Indian, and Pakistani stars dominated.

That changed in 2010, when England won their first men's ICC trophy - the T20 World Cup in the West Indies - with Paul Collingwood's team defeating Australia in the final. A decade later, Eoin Morgan's side, packed with aggressive hitters and mystery spinners, used the lessons of T20 to win the 2019 ODI World Cup and the 2022 T20 World Cup.

On the women's side, England won the inaugural Women's T20 World Cup in 2009, setting the standard for professionalism and inspiring a new generation of female cricketers.

The Style of Play

T20 didn't just shorten the game; it changed how cricket is played:

- **Power-hitting** became an art form - Chris Gayle, AB de Villiers, Brendon McCullum, and more turned six-hitting into routine.
- **Death bowling** -Yorkers, slower balls, wide Yorkers - became as valuable as a century.
- **Fielding standards** soared; acrobatic boundary catches became T20 trademarks.
- **Innovation** - ramps, scoops, switch-hits redefined batting.

The influence spilled over into Tests, too. Modern Test cricket, from Ben Stokes' Headingley miracle to Bazball's all-out attack, owes much to the fearless, fast-scoring mindset born in T20.

Modern T20: The Power and the Debate

Today, T20 is the dominant commercial format of the game. IPL contracts are worth millions. Players like Rashid Khan, Kieron Pollard, and Andre Russell have built careers almost entirely around franchise cricket. Crowds for domestic leagues often outstrip Test attendances.

But the rise of T20 has sparked debate:

- Has it damaged Test cricket by pulling players away?

- Has the lure of money unbalanced the sport?

- Or has it saved cricket by attracting a new generation of fans?

For many, the answer is both. T20 is divisive but vital. It funds the grassroots, keeps cricket on screens worldwide, and provides unforgettable entertainment, even as it challenges the game's traditional rhythms.

The Format That Changed Everything

What began as an experiment on a chilly English evening in 2003 has become the beating heart of world cricket. T20 didn't just give cricket a new format; it gave it new life. It created household names, global leagues, and moments of magic from Carlos Brathwaite's "Remember the name!" sixes in 2016 to Jos Buttler scooping Australia for six at the MCG.

It is loud, it is brash, it is commercial, but it is also cricket's greatest modern success story. Love it or hate it, T20 is here to stay.

CHAPTER THIRTY-SIX: THE HUNDRED

Reinventing the English Summer

A Radical New Idea

By the start of the 21st century, county cricket was both rich in heritage and weighed down by it. The County Championship still produced England's Test stars, but long matches on damp April mornings struggled to hold the attention of casual fans. Even the T20 Blast, a roaring success when it was launched in 2003, began to lose ground internationally as the Indian Premier League and Australia's Big Bash pulled in global audiences, glitz, and money.

The ECB faced a dilemma. The counties were the bedrock of English cricket, but could they deliver the crowds, sponsorship, and television spectacle needed to secure the game's future? Something bolder was required something that would cut through the noise of modern sport and entertainment.

The solution was radical: create a new competition altogether, with new teams, new branding, and even a new format. Shorter, sharper, built for television, and pitched directly at families and younger fans who might never step inside a county ground.

Traditionalists bristled. Purists muttered. But in 2021, after a pandemic delay, the gamble was finally rolled out.

England's cricket summer had a new sound, the crack of bat and ball timed not by overs but by a countdown clock. Neon kits replaced blazers, mascots danced on the boundary, and men's and women's matches were played side by side on equal terms.

This was The Hundred: cricket's most daring experiment in generations.

The Format

- **100 balls per innings**: a team faces 100 legal deliveries, with a change of ends after every 10 balls.

- **Bowlers**: each can deliver a maximum of 20 balls, either in sets of 5 or 10.

- **Powerplay**: first 25 balls of the innings with only two fielders outside the 30-yard circle.

- **Match length**: around 2 hours 30 minutes, shorter than most T20 matches, making it more family friendly.

- **Innovation**: simple graphics, countdown clocks, on-field DJs, fireworks, cricket repackaged as prime-time entertainment.

The Teams

Unlike county cricket, The Hundred is based on eight new, city-based franchises designed to attract wider, regional fanbases rather than just county loyalties. Each side fields both a men's and women's team, playing on the same day at the same ground a landmark first in professional cricket.

1. **Birmingham Phoenix – based at Edgbaston.**
2. **London Spirit – Lord's, representing the capital.**
3. **Manchester Originals – Old Trafford.**
4. **Northern Superchargers – Headingley, Leeds.**
5. **Oval Invincibles – The Oval, South London.**
6. **Southern Brave – Southampton's Ageas Bowl.**
7. **Trent Rockets – Trent Bridge, Nottingham.**
8. **Welsh Fire – Sophia Gardens, Cardiff.**

Each squad is built through a player draft, a concept borrowed from the IPL, ensuring an even spread of England internationals, overseas stars, and homegrown talent.

Why the Hundred Was Different

- **Men's and Women's Equality**: for the first time in a major tournament, women's matches were given equal billing, broadcast on prime channels with the same branding and promotion.

- **Free-to-Air TV**: matches shown on both Sky Sports and BBC; the first-time live men's cricket had been on free TV in the UK since 2005.

- **Family Focus**: shorter games, affordable tickets for kids, and entertainment designed to feel like a festival.

- **Overseas Stars**: players like Rashid Khan, Smriti Mandhana, Trent Boult, and Ellyse Perry brought global appeal.

The Controversy

The Hundred has not been without critics. Traditional fans argued that the ECB should have built on the Blast rather than invent a new format. Some counties feared they were being sidelined in favour of "city cricket." Others worried about the dilution of red-ball cricket.

But the ECB's gamble has paid off in part: record TV audiences, big family crowds, and a surge in visibility for women's cricket. Young fans now know team names like "Oval Invincibles" before they learn the difference between Yorkshire and Surrey.

Notable Moments

- **2021**: The first men's champions were the Southern Brave, while the women's title went to the Oval Invincibles.

- **2022**: Trent Rockets' men and Oval Invincibles' women triumphed.

- **2023**: Southern Brave's men regained the title; Oval Invincibles completed a women's hat-trick.

- Standout stars included Moeen Ali, Ben Stokes, Sam Curran, Dane van Niekerk, and Lauren Winfield-Hill.

Fan Culture: Fancy Dress, Fireworks, and Families

If county cricket is a flask of tea and a notebook of bowling figures, The Hundred is a festival with cricket in the middle of it. Fireworks greet every six. DJs spin tracks between overs. Kids wave foam fingers and wear glow-in-the-dark face paint.

Each ground has developed quirks:

- At Edgbaston, the Hollies Stand fizzes with fancy dress (from Elvis to inflatable bananas).

- At Cardiff, dragon costumes and Welsh songs echo over the River Taff.

- At Headingley, the Superchargers faithful bring football chants into cricket: "We all hate Lancashire!" makes an appearance more than once.

- At the Oval, Invincibles fans lean into London pride, turning games into mini street parties.

The Hundred's greatest success has been drawing in new fans: kids who never saw a County Championship scorecard, families who thought cricket was too slow, and women who feel included in equal-billing double-headers.

The Hundred Today

Three seasons in, The Hundred is firmly part of the English summer. Crowds at Lord's, Headingley, and Edgbaston have swelled with new demographics. More families, more women, and more kids in replica kits.

The ECB sees it as crucial for the game's future finances, with sponsorships, TV deals, and merchandise helping sustain grassroots projects and county structures.

Yet the debate continues: is The Hundred the future of cricket, or just a flashy sideshow? For now, it remains a lightning rod for discussion but one that has undeniably given cricket a new energy.

The Hundred may never win over every traditionalist, but its boldness cannot be ignored. In an age where attention spans are short, the competition has delivered a product that's short, sharp, and colourful while putting men's and women's cricket side by side in a way no other competition has.

In many ways, The Hundred is cricket's latest great experiment, one that may define how the game survives and thrives in the 21st century.

CHAPTER THIRTY-SEVEN: THE COUNTY CHAMPIONSHIP

Four Days of Tradition, Skill, and Strategy

When people talk about cricket in England, Test matches usually take the headlines. But behind the scenes, away from the TV razzmatazz of white-ball tournaments and the packed crowds of The Hundred, sits the County Championship, the beating heart of the English game. It is here, across the eighteen counties of England and Wales, that players hone their craft, reputations are built, and Test heroes are born. For traditionalists, the Championship is cricket in its purest form: four days, a red ball, and endless possibilities.

The Origins of County Cricket

The roots of county cricket stretch back to the 18th century, when matches between counties like Kent, Surrey, and Sussex were already common. Gambling often drove these contests, with aristocrats putting down heavy wagers, but they also sowed the seeds for county pride.

By the mid-19th century, county sides were formalising into professional outfits. Yorkshire County Cricket Club (founded 1863) and Lancashire (1864) were among the pioneers, and fierce rivalries quickly emerged. The Roses Match, Yorkshire vs Lancashire, soon became one of English sport's most bitter and famous rivalries, a north vs north-west struggle that drew huge crowds.

The first official County Championship was staged in 1890, with Surrey being the inaugural winners. Since then, it has been the annual proving ground for England's best cricketers.

The Format – Four Days of Patience and Drama

Unlike the flashy formats of T20 or The Hundred, the County Championship demands endurance and skill across four days. Each side has two innings, and the match can end in a win, a draw, or a rare tie. The length means tactics are layered and nuanced:

· Captains must manage bowlers to keep them fresh across 90 overs a day.

· Batters must dig in, often playing through tough sessions against the new ball.

· Weather, so often an English factor, can turn a winning position into a frustrating draw.

The scoring system has evolved over the years, rewarding wins but also giving bonus points for batting and bowling performances, to keep the table competitive.

Divisions and Modern Structure

Today, the Championship is split into two divisions (introduced in 2000), with promotion and relegation between them. This has added spice to the competition, with counties fighting not only for the title but to avoid the drop.

Counties also play matches at out-grounds as well as their main stadiums. So, you might see Yorkshire playing at Scarborough by the sea, or Somerset at Taunton surrounded by cider orchards, settings that give the Championship its distinctly English charm.

The Championship as a Test Match Nursery

For England's Test side, the County Championship is the nursery of champions. Almost every great Test player cut their teeth in four-day county cricket:

· **Jack Hobbs** (Surrey) – the "Master" of English batting.

· **Len Hutton** (Yorkshire) – who scored 364 in a Test at The Oval, still England's highest Test score.

- **Ian Botham** (Somerset) – swashbuckling all-rounder who lit up county grounds before taking on the world.

- **Alastair Cook** (Essex) – England's record Test run-scorer, forged in county matches.

- **James Anderson** (Lancashire) – learned his craft swinging the red ball at Old Trafford.

For bowlers especially, the four-day game is essential. Bowling 20 overs a day, adjusting to changing pitches, and attacking over multiple spells, it's where skills are sharpened for the Test arena.

Famous County Championship Stories

The Championship has provided some of English cricket's most enduring tales:

- **Brian Lara's 501 not out (1994, Warwickshire)** – the highest first-class score in history, made at Edgbaston.

- **Somerset's near-miss in 2010** – finishing runners-up in all three domestic competitions, the heartbreak summed up by their failure to clinch the Championship on the last day.

- **Yorkshire dominance (1960s)** – winning seven titles in ten years under Brian Close and Ray Illingworth.

- **Essex's golden age (1979–1992)** – led by Graham Gooch, Essex became a powerhouse of English cricket.

County Championship Crowds and Culture

Unlike the vibrant, noisy crowds of T20 nights, Championship cricket has a different rhythm. Fans bring newspapers, picnic baskets, and thermos flasks. Many are long-time members who take the same seats year after year. The atmosphere is more contemplative – you can hear conversations in the stands, but there's real passion for the nuances of the game.

Scarborough Festival, for example, is an annual highlight. Thousands flock to the seaside ground, mixing deckchairs with chants of "Yorkshire, Yorkshire," and a fairground feel. These festivals keep the Championship rooted in community spirit.

Challenges in the Modern Era

In truth, the County Championship has struggled for mainstream attention in the era of T20 leagues and The Hundred. Matches often clash with school or work, limiting live attendances. Media coverage has also declined compared to the past.

Yet, the Championship retains fierce loyalty. Purists argue it is the soul of English cricket, the format that prepares players for the mental and technical demands of Test cricket. Even England captains Joe Root, Ben Stokes and Alastair Cook have stressed that without the Championship, the Test team would wither.

Women's Four-Day Cricket?

While women's domestic cricket in England has focused more on limited-overs formats (like the Rachael Heyhoe Flint Trophy and Charlotte Edwards Cup), there is growing debate about reviving or creating a women's multi-day county or regional championship. Many players, including England's Heather Knight, have expressed the desire to play more long-format cricket to prepare for women's Test matches. This may be the next chapter in the evolution of the Championship ethos.

Why the County Championship Still Matters

For those who truly love the game, the Championship is more than just another competition. It is a reminder that cricket is about patience as much as power, about endurance as much as entertainment. It is about the art of leaving a ball well outside off stump, or a bowler crafting a dismissal over ten overs of probing accuracy.

The Championship is the thread that links village cricket to the Test arena, from Headingley to Taunton, from Chester-le-Street to Hove. It remains the purest domestic form of the game, a place where reputations are forged, history is written, and cricket's timeless rhythms play out over four patient, glorious days.

PART FIVE

CHAPTER THIRTY-EIGHT: THE MARYLEBONE CRICKET CLUB (MCC)

Origins and Early Years

The Marylebone Cricket Club (MCC) is one of the most famous sporting institutions in the world, and arguably the most influential in cricket's long history. Founded in 1787, it began life when Thomas Lord, a businessman and professional cricketer, established a new cricket ground in Marylebone, London. This ground, known initially as Lord's, became the MCC's home, and remains so today.

From the very beginning, MCC positioned itself as cricket's custodian. In 1788, just a year after its creation, it published a revised version of the Laws of Cricket, setting itself apart from other clubs by assuming responsibility for codifying the rules of the game. This authority was recognised across England and eventually across the cricketing world.

The MCC and the Laws of Cricket

For more than two centuries, the MCC has been the official guardian of the Laws of Cricket. Every amendment, revision, or addition to the Laws had to pass through MCC committees, often after much debate. For example:

- In 1835, MCC codified the round-arm bowling revolution, which had split cricketing opinion.

- Later, they oversaw the transition to overarm bowling in 1864.

- In the 20th century, MCC committees tackled issues such as dangerous bowling and player safety. Limited-overs cricket, however, was introduced by English cricket authorities outside the MCC.

Even today, while the International Cricket Council (ICC) governs the global game, the MCC remains the official custodian of the Laws, a rare case of a private club holding sway over an international sport. The ICC sets the Playing Conditions for international matches, but the Laws themselves remain under MCC control.

The Ground: Lord's

MCC is inseparable from its famous home ground, Lord's Cricket Ground in St John's Wood, London. Known as the "Home of Cricket," Lord's is steeped in history:

- It hosted its first match in 1814 at the current site.
- The Pavilion, with its Long Room, is an iconic part of cricketing heritage.
- Lord's has staged countless historic matches, from Test debuts to World Cup finals.

The ground also houses the MCC Museum, which holds priceless cricketing artefacts, including The Ashes urn, perhaps the most famous trophy in cricket.

Culture and Traditions

For most of its history, MCC was an elite and exclusive club. Its members, dressed in the famous bacon-and-egg striped blazers (red and yellow), became a symbol of cricketing authority. Players at Lord's traditionally enter the field through the Long Room, lined with portraits of past greats, where MCC members in ties and jackets applaud them, one of sport's most unusual and atmospheric walks.

Until 1968, MCC effectively ran English cricket, selecting England's Test teams and organising overseas tours. After governance shifted to the newly formed TCCB (later the ECB), MCC continued to manage some touring arrangements for a few years. The final England side officially described as an "MCC team" was the 1976–77 tour of India. After that, all England teams toured under the ECB's authority, even though MCC continued to play an influential ceremonial and custodial role.

Membership and How to Join

Membership of the MCC has always been highly sought after, and for much of its history, extremely exclusive:

- **Waiting list**: The club has had a waiting list stretching up to 30 years. Many apply in childhood and only gain admission in middle age.

- **Nomination**: Prospective members must be nominated by existing members.

- **Election**: Successful candidates are elected following committee approval.

- **Categories**: Full membership brings rights to use the Pavilion, vote on club matters, and buy tickets to Lord's Test matches. Associate and temporary memberships also exist.

In the past, membership was almost entirely male and upper-class. Women were not admitted as members until 1999, after decades of campaigning led most famously by Rachael Heyhoe Flint, former England captain. The decision marked a huge cultural shift for the club, which had been seen as one of the last bastions of male sporting privilege.

MCC Today

The MCC's role has changed with the rise of the ICC and national boards, but it remains deeply significant:

- It continues as the guardian of the Laws of Cricket.

- It runs Lord's Cricket Ground, hosting Tests, ODIs, The Hundred, and county fixtures.

- It maintains an active playing programme: MCC teams tour the world, often to promote cricket in developing nations.

- It invests in cricketing infrastructure and coaching worldwide, supporting the game at grassroots and international level.

The club has also worked to modernise its image. It has diversified its membership, become more inclusive, and seeks to project itself as a living custodian rather than a relic of Victorian elitism.

Legacy and Symbolism

For over two centuries, MCC has embodied cricket's traditions, for good and ill. Critics argue it was too slow to adapt, barring women until 1999, clinging to class privilege, and resisting reforms. Yet its contributions are undeniable: without MCC, cricket may never have had a single set of codified laws, nor the same sense of shared history.

The MCC's famous motto *"Spirit of Cricket"* sums up its ongoing mission. More than any other club, MCC seeks to remind players, officials, and fans that cricket is about more than winning it is about fairness, respect, and honour.

Summary

- **Founded**: 1787 by Thomas Lord.

- **Key role**: Guardian of the Laws of Cricket.

- **Historic base**: Lord's Cricket Ground (since 1814).

- **Traditions:** Iconic Pavilion, Long Room, egg-and-bacon blazers.

- **Membership**: Long waiting list, historically male-only, women admitted in 1999.

- **Modern role**: Still custodian of the Laws; runs Lord's; promotes cricket worldwide.

CHAPTER THIRTY-NINE: THE INTERNATIONAL CRICKET COUNCIL (ICC)

The Origins – From Imperial to International

Cricket, for all its timeless traditions, has often lagged behind in building global structures. For much of its early history, the game's administration rested in the hands of the Marylebone Cricket Club (MCC), the guardians of the Laws of Cricket. But by the early 20th century, with more nations playing Test matches and the sport spreading beyond England's colonial reach, the need for a more formal governing body became obvious.

In 1909, the Imperial Cricket Conference was formed by England, Australia, and South Africa. The name reflected the times: this was still very much a game run by and for the old dominions of the British Empire. India, New Zealand, and the West Indies joined in 1926, and Pakistan followed after independence in 1953.

It wasn't until 1965 that the conference shed its "Imperial" tag, becoming the International Cricket Conference, and finally, in 1989, the International Cricket Council (ICC). That evolution symbolised cricket's shift from a colonial pastime to a truly global sport.

What the ICC Does

The ICC today is cricket's world governing body, headquartered in Dubai, overseeing more than 100 member nations. Of these, 12 are Full Members with Test status (England, Australia, India, Pakistan, New Zealand, South Africa, West Indies, Sri Lanka, Bangladesh, Zimbabwe, Afghanistan, and Ireland), while the rest are Associate Members, developing the game at different levels.

Its core responsibilities include:

- **Global Governance:** Setting rules, codes of conduct, and disciplinary standards. While the MCC still officially owns the Laws of Cricket, the ICC regulates how they are applied internationally.

- **Tournaments:** Running world events like the Cricket World Cup (ODI), the T20 World Cup, and the World Test Championship.

- **Rankings & Fixtures:** Maintaining official world rankings across formats and coordinating international calendars to avoid clashes.

- **Anti-Corruption** & Integrity: Through its Anti-Corruption Unit (ACU), the ICC works to combat match-fixing and betting scandals.

- **Umpiring & Technology:** Training and appointing elite umpires and managing the use of Decision Review System (DRS), Hawk-Eye, and other technologies.

- **Development:** Supporting Associate nations with funding, coaching, and infrastructure to grow the game globally.

The Powerhouses and Politics

No chapter on the ICC would be complete without addressing the elephant in the room: politics.

While the ICC is meant to be a collective of equal voices, the financial clout of the "Big Three" India, England, and Australia, has often dominated proceedings. India's Board of Control for Cricket (BCCI) in particular now wields huge influence due to the financial boom of the IPL and its massive broadcasting markets. Critics argue that this creates an imbalance, with smaller nations struggling for equal opportunities, especially in scheduling Test matches.

At the same time, the ICC has faced challenges balancing the needs of its Full Members with its ambitious goal of globalising the game. For example, Afghanistan's rise to Full Member status has been celebrated, while nations such as the Netherlands, Scotland, and Namibia push for more chances on the big stage.

The ICC Tournaments – Cricket's Global Festivals

The ICC is perhaps best known to fans for its tournaments:

- **Cricket World Cup (ODI)** – first held in 1975 in England, it remains the sport's biggest showcase event.

- **T20 World Cup** – launched in 2007, it has become a blockbuster, with shorter games attracting new audiences.

- **Champions Trophy** – often called the "mini-World Cup," though its future has been uncertain.

- **World Test Championship** – the newest jewel, introduced in 2019 to give Test cricket a structured global competition.

- **Women's ICC Tournaments** – including the Women's ODI and T20 World Cups, both of which have grown rapidly in profile, especially since Australia's dominance and India's emergence as a powerhouse.

For Associate nations, events like the ICC Men's T20 World Cup Qualifiers and the Cricket World Cup League provide crucial exposure and opportunities to compete with the best.

Women's Cricket and the ICC

In 2005, the ICC merged with the International Women's Cricket Council (IWCC), bringing women's cricket under its umbrella. This was a landmark moment, ensuring that women's cricket had access to the same resources, development structures, and marketing reach as the men's game.

Since then, the ICC has expanded the Women's World Cup, introduced the Women's T20 World Cup, and worked with domestic boards to encourage professionalism. The decision to put women's World Cup finals in major stadiums, like the MCG in 2020, where over 86,000 fans watched Australia play India, showed the enormous potential of the women's game under ICC stewardship.

The Critics

The ICC is not without controversy:

- Critics accuse it of being too commercially driven, prioritising broadcast revenue over the balance of formats.

- Test cricket's place is often seen as threatened, with many accusing the ICC of favouring T20 for financial reasons.

- Associates argue they are sidelined, with only a handful of nations enjoying regular access to the biggest tournaments.

Yet despite the criticism, it remains the only body capable of holding the game together globally.

Beyond the Elites – The ICC's Role in Grassroots & Disability Cricket

While the ICC is often seen through the glitz of World Cups and the high-stakes politics of Test nations, one of its most important roles is far less glamorous but arguably more impactful: growing the game at every level.

Disability Cricket – Making the Game for Everyone

The ICC supports and recognises disability cricket globally, although the official governance of blind, deaf, physical disability, and learning disability formats is led by specialist organisations such as the World Blind Cricket Council, Deaf International Cricket Council, and national boards like the ECB.

England, Australia, India, South Africa, and Pakistan have been leading lights, staging World Cups and bilateral series across different disability formats. The ICC helps provide governance, funding channels, and official recognition so that disability cricket isn't just "charity sport" but serious, competitive cricket played with national pride.

Highlights include:

· The Blind Cricket World Cup, organised by the World Blind Cricket Council, is recognised and supported by the ICC through promotional and development initiatives.

· The Physical Disability World Cup (2015) was organised by national boards with ICC support and recognition.

· The introduction of disability cricketers into promotional campaigns and awareness weeks, ensuring visibility on the global stage.

By giving its platform, the ICC signals that a blind batter timing a drive by sound or a bowler running in with a prosthetic leg is every bit as much a cricketer as Joe Root or Virat Kohli.

Women's Pathways and Equality

The ICC's decision in 2005 to merge with the International Women's Cricket Council (IWCC) wasn't just administrative. It symbolised a turning point in how cricket viewed women's participation. The ICC now:

· Runs Women's ODI and T20 World Cups, with equal branding and global broadcasting deals.

· Sets minimum prize-money standards, which it has steadily increased to narrow the gap with the men's game.

· Ensures women's cricket has equal footing in rankings, records, and global tournaments.

The result? Women's cricket is no longer a sidenote. The ICC has made it an integral part of cricket's future, inspiring a new generation of fans and players.

Global Expansion – Beyond the 12 Full Members

For all its focus on the established cricketing giants, the ICC has 96 Associate Members, nations where cricket is still finding its roots. The ICC invests heavily in these through:

- **Development grants** for infrastructure, pitches, and equipment.

- **Coach education** programmes to help raise standards.

- **Regional tournaments** such as the ICC Men's and Women's T20 World Cup Qualifiers.

- **Pathway to the top:** allowing Associate nations to reach the global stage.

This has already borne fruit:

- Afghanistan and Ireland moved from Associate to Full Member status, now playing Test cricket.

- Teams like Nepal, Scotland, Namibia, and the Netherlands have beaten major nations in ICC tournaments, proving cricket's growing competitive balance.

- The 2024 Men's T20 World Cup in the USA and West Indies showed how cricket can capture new audiences in non-traditional regions.

Grassroots Inspiration

At the foundation of it all is the belief that cricket must remain accessible. The ICC works with the Lord's Taverners, Chance to Shine, and other partner charities to encourage school programmes, particularly in places where children may not otherwise pick up a bat.

It also promotes Tape Ball Cricket in South Asia, Beach Cricket in the Caribbean, and Street Cricket in South America and Africa, recognising that cricket doesn't always need whites, manicured outfields, and grand pavilions. It can be played anywhere, by anyone.

CONCLUSION – A GLOBAL GAME FOR ALL

The ICC may sometimes be criticised for being commercial or political, but behind the headlines it has helped turn cricket from a colonial pastime into a truly global sport.

Without it, there would be no World Cups, no World Test Championship, no structured anti-corruption framework, and little chance for smaller nations to rise. With it, cricket has the chance to be both a global sport and a global business.

At its best, the ICC embodies the spirit of the game: ensuring cricket is fair, competitive, and open to all. At its worst, it reflects the politics and inequalities of the world it governs. But for better or worse, the ICC is the glue that binds together cricket's diverse family, from Headingley to Harare, Mumbai to Melbourne, and Dubai to Dublin.

Its support for disability cricket ensures that nobody is excluded. Its investment in women's cricket has given the game half of its future. Its development programmes ensure that a boy in Kabul, a girl in Nairobi, or a deaf cricketer in Cape Town can all see a pathway to the top.

In many ways, the ICC's greatest achievement isn't the World Cup trophies or the billion-dollar TV deals. It is the simple truth that cricket, whether in the bright lights of the MCG or on a dusty schoolyard in Nepal, belongs to everyone.

CHAPTER FORTY: THE ENGLAND AND WALES CRICKET BOARD (ECB)

The Beginning of a Modern Governing Body

The England and Wales Cricket Board (ECB) is the organisation that runs cricket in England and Wales. It is the authority behind every match played under its jurisdiction, from grassroots club games on village greens to England's men's and women's national teams competing at Lord's, the Oval, or on the world stage. But the ECB has not always existed.

Before its creation in 1997, the administration of cricket in England was somewhat fragmented. Three separate bodies ran the game:

· **The Test and County Cricket Board (TCCB)** – which managed the professional men's game, including county cricket and the England men's Test team.

· **The National Cricket Association (NCA)** – which was responsible for the amateur and grassroots game.

· **The Cricket Council** – a coordinating committee that oversaw overall policy but had limited direct power.

By the 1990s, it was clear that this fragmented structure was holding the game back. Other sports, like football and rugby, had streamlined governing bodies that could negotiate sponsorships, organise competitions, and promote development more effectively. Cricket needed a single, unified organisation.

And so, in January 1997, the England and Wales Cricket Board was born. It replaced the TCCB, NCA, and Cricket Council, becoming the sole governing body of cricket in England and Wales. For the first time, the professional and recreational sides of the sport were brought under one roof.

What the ECB Does

The ECB is a vast organisation with responsibilities stretching across every level of the game. At its core, it exists to develop cricket, grow participation, and ensure the success of England's national teams.

Its main roles include:

· **Running England's Men's**, **Women's, Disability** (Deaf, Learning Disability, and Physical Disability), and Age-Group teams, and supporting the England Blind team within the World Blind Cricket Council structure.

· **Organising Domestic Competitions** – including the County Championship, Vitality Blast, Royal London One-Day Cup, The Hundred, and women's tournaments like the Rachael Heyhoe Flint Trophy and Charlotte Edwards Cup.

· **Grassroots Development** – funding local clubs, schools' programmes, and entry-level initiatives such as All Stars and Dynamos Cricket.

· **Inclusivity and Disability Cricket** – building strong pathways for Blind, Deaf, Learning Disability, and Physical Disability cricket.

· **Coach, Umpire, and Official Development** – training and certifying thousands of volunteers and professionals each year.

· **Funding and Commercial Growth** – negotiating broadcasting rights and sponsorship deals, with income reinvested back into counties and grassroots.

Women's and Disability Cricket

A major achievement of the ECB has been the professionalisation of women's cricket. In 2014, it awarded the first central contracts to England Women, a landmark moment that helped secure England's World Cup triumph in 2017. In 2020, professional contracts were extended to domestic women's players for the first time.

Disability cricket is also a priority, with England competing strongly in Blind, Deaf, Learning Disability, and Physical Disability formats. These teams are run by the

ECB, while most international disability tournaments are organised by partner bodies such as the World Blind Cricket Council or national boards.

Innovation – The Hundred

The ECB's boldest recent initiative has been The Hundred, launched in 2021. With 100-ball innings, city-based franchises, men's and women's matches are played on equal billing in double-header format, with shared branding and marketing, and a family-friendly emphasis, it was designed to attract a new audience.

Recent Challenges and Controversies

Despite its successes, the ECB has faced some of the most testing periods in its history in recent years.

· **Racism and Discrimination Scandals:** In 2021, former Yorkshire cricketer Azeem Rafiq gave testimony that exposed a culture of racism in parts of English cricket. His evidence before Parliament triggered widespread criticism of the ECB's handling of discrimination. The Independent Commission for Equity in Cricket published its report in June 2023, concluding that racism is entrenched, and that sexism, elitism, and class-based discrimination persist across parts of the game.

· **Financial Pressures**: Like many sports bodies, the ECB was hit hard by the COVID-19 pandemic. With matches played behind closed doors in 2020, revenues collapsed. Emergency loans and cost-cutting measures followed, with some counties struggling to survive. The ECB continues to balance the need for financial stability with investment in the grassroots and women's game.

· **Balancing Tradition and Modernity**: The introduction of The Hundred has divided opinion. Supporters praise it as a lifeline for the sport in attracting younger audiences; critics argue it threatens the identity of county cricket. Managing this tension between innovation and heritage remains one of the ECB's biggest challenges.

· **Fixture Congestion**: With Tests, ODIs, T20Is, The Hundred, county cricket, and global franchise tournaments, the cricket calendar has become overcrowded. The ECB faces increasing pressure from players, coaches, and fans to simplify schedules while maintaining revenue streams.

Notable ECB Leaders and Chairs

The ECB's direction has often reflected the personalities and priorities of its leaders:

· **Lord MacLaurin (1997–2002)** – The ECB's first chair, MacLaurin oversaw the unification of cricket's governing structures and set the foundations for central contracts for England players.

· **David Morgan (2002–2007)** – A steady influence who later became ICC President, he helped stabilise the ECB after a turbulent early period.

· **Giles Clarke (2007–2015)** – A controversial but influential figure, Clarke was instrumental in driving commercial revenues, particularly through TV deals, but was often criticised for his combative style.

· **Colin Graves (2015–2020)** – Known for pushing modernisation, Graves backed The Hundred and pushed counties towards financial reform. He also clashed with traditionalists who accused him of neglecting Test and county cricket.

· **Ian Watmore (2020–2021)** – resigned amid facing criticism from the cancelled Pakistan tour, combined with wider pressure on the ECB during the post-COVID period

· **Richard Thompson (2022–present)** – A former Surrey chairman, Thompson has focused on repairing trust, tackling discrimination, and making the ECB more transparent and inclusive.

These leaders have shaped everything from broadcasting deals and grassroots investment to international competitiveness and inclusivity. Each has left their mark, for better or worse on the modern game.

The Future of the ECB

The ECB's vision is summed up in one phrase: "Cricket is a game for everyone." Its future success depends on whether it can deliver on this promise. This means:

· Making cricket genuinely inclusive and free from discrimination.

· Growing the women's game further, building on the momentum of World Cups and The Hundred.

· Protecting Test cricket and the County Championship while keeping the sport financially viable.

· Expanding cricket into schools and diverse communities, ensuring the next generation picks up a bat or ball.

CONCLUSION

Since its creation in 1997, the ECB has modernised cricket in England and Wales, uniting the professional and amateur sides of the game under one umbrella. It has delivered international success, professionalised women's cricket, and pioneered new formats like The Hundred.

But it has also been tested by racism scandals, financial struggles, and the constant battle to balance tradition with innovation. How it responds to these challenges will shape not just the future of English cricket, but the game's role in society.

For all its controversies, one truth remains clear: the ECB is the heartbeat of cricket in England and Wales, and its decisions will define the game for generations to come.

CHAPTER FORTY-ONE: THE LORD'S TAVERNERS

Origins – From Pub Banter to National Charity

The Lord's Taverners began not in the Pavilion at Lord's, but in a nearby pub. In the late 1940s, a group of actors, journalists, and cricket enthusiasts used to meet at the Tavern bar at Lord's Cricket Ground. They gathered to watch cricket, share drinks, and indulge in light-hearted cricket talk.

In 1950, this informal gathering was formalised into a club called the Lord's Taverners, with the idea that cricket could be used as a force for good in society. The club was initially a social organisation of entertainers and sports lovers but quickly developed a charitable mission: to give young people, especially those facing disadvantage or disability, opportunities to play and enjoy sport.

Its first president was the actor Jack Warner, star of the *Dixon of Dock Green* TV series. Other early members included theatrical and sporting personalities who combined a love of showbusiness with a passion for cricket.

Purpose and Mission

The Lord's Taverners' central belief has always been that sport, and cricket in particular, can transform young lives. From its early days, the club raised money to support youth cricket and disability sport, and it grew into the UK's leading cricket and disability sport charity.

Its work focuses on:
- **Disadvantaged and disabled young people** – providing chances to access sport when other opportunities may be denied.

- **Table Cricket** – a game invented in the 1990s that allows young people with physical or learning disabilities to play cricket on a table-top, using adapted equipment. The Taverners run a national Table Cricket competition involving thousands of children across schools and community centres.

- **Wicketz** – a community cricket programme for young people living in deprived areas, using cricket as a tool to promote life skills, teamwork, and confidence.

- **Equipment and transport** – over decades, the charity has supplied thousands of specially adapted minibuses, known as "green buses," to schools, youth clubs, and disability organisations. These vehicles have become an iconic symbol of the Lord's Taverners' work.

Activities and Fundraising

The Taverners have always mixed cricket with entertainment. Their fundraising activities include:

- **Celebrity cricket matches** – featuring actors, comedians, and ex-professional cricketers.

- **Annual dinners and lunches** – famous for their speeches, humour, and auctions.

- **Golf days, concerts, and gala events** – blending sport and showbiz to raise funds.

They also host special days at Lord's and other grounds, bringing children from disadvantaged backgrounds to experience a day of cricket at the highest level.

Notable Supporters and Presidents

The Lord's Taverners has attracted a wide range of famous supporters over the years:

- Prince Philip, Duke of Edinburgh, became the charity's patron in 1950 and remained involved for decades.

- Sir John Mills, Eric Morecambe, Ronnie Corbett, Henry Cooper, Richard Briers, and other well-known entertainers served as presidents or prominent members.

- Many former professional cricketers, including England captains, have supported the cause.

- In recent years, figures like David Gower and Chris Tarrant have been associated with the club's leadership.

This blend of celebrity, humour, and cricketing gravitas has made Taverners events both popular and effective fundraisers.

How to Join

The Lord's Taverners operates as a membership organisation. Anyone with a passion for cricket and a commitment to the charity's mission can apply.

Membership types:

- **Full Membership**: open to men and women, offering the chance to attend events, vote at meetings, and take part in Taverners' activities.

- **Regional Membership**: there are local branches across the UK, so members can join fundraising and social events in their area.

- **Corporate Membership**: companies can affiliate and support the charity while engaging staff and clients in events.

Application process:

- Prospective members apply via the Lord's Taverners' official website.

- Annual subscriptions help fund charitable activities.

- Members are encouraged to attend events, volunteer, and act as ambassadors for the charity's work.

The club's welcoming ethos contrasts with the exclusivity of institutions like the MCC: while still maintaining traditions, the Taverners emphasise community, fun, and making a difference.

Lord's Taverners Today

Now, more than 70 years after its founding, the Lord's Taverners has evolved from a group of cricket-loving actors in a bar into a major UK charity. Each year, it invests millions of pounds in programmes that give children across the country the chance to enjoy the benefits of sport.

- **Table Cricket** involves over 10,000 young people annually.

- The **Wicketz programme** runs in more than a dozen UK cities, reaching children in some of the country's most deprived communities.

- Over 1,300 green minibuses have been donated since the 1970s.

The Taverners remain a unique blend of cricket, comedy, and charity: a reminder that sport at its best is not only about competition but about inclusion, joy, and shared opportunity.

Summary

- **Founded**: 1950, at the Tavern bar in Lord's.

- **Mission**: Use cricket and sport to help disadvantaged and disabled young people.

- **Work**: Table Cricket, Wicketz, minibuses, and equipment.

- **Fundraising**: Celebrity cricket, gala dinners, charity events.

- **Membership**: Open to all, with regional and corporate options.

- **Legacy**: Over 70 years of changing lives through cricket.

CHAPTER FORTY-TWO: COUNTY CRICKET BOARDS

The Birth of County Cricket

County cricket is at the heart of English cricket. The very first county sides began forming in the 18th and 19th centuries, when matches between local clubs and regions grew in popularity. By 1890, the County Championship was officially established, with counties competing for the title each summer.

The oldest county clubs, such as Sussex (founded 1839), Surrey (1845), and Yorkshire (1863) were set up by groups of cricketing enthusiasts, landowners, and early professionals. Over time, they evolved into professional sporting organisations.

Today, there are 18 First-Class County Clubs in England and Wales.

Who Are They and What Do They Do?

County clubs are professional teams responsible for developing and showcasing cricket in their regions. Their main roles include:

- **Playing professional cricket** – They compete in the County Championship (red-ball), the One-Day Cup, and the T20 Blast.

- **Developing talent** – They run academies and youth programmes to identify and train the next generation of cricketers.

- **Community outreach** – County clubs often run coaching sessions, school programmes, and grassroots cricket schemes to encourage wider participation.

- **Providing pathways** – For young players, county cricket is the main stepping stone to professional cricket and ultimately to playing for England.

How Do They Choose Players?

Counties recruit players in a number of ways:

- **Academies** – Talented youngsters are scouted through schools, clubs, and trials, and nurtured through county academies.

- **Second XI cricket** – Promising players can prove themselves in reserve matches before breaking into the first team.

- **Transfers** – Experienced professionals can move between counties.

- **Overseas signings** – Counties may bring in international stars to strengthen their squads, especially for T20 cricket.

- **Draft systems** – In competitions like *The Hundred*, players are selected via a national draft rather than county affiliation.

Cricket Boards: The Wider Structure

While county clubs focus on professional cricket, county cricket boards (like the Yorkshire Cricket Board, YCB)[3] are responsible for the grassroots game.

The YCB, for example, oversees cricket at every level below the professional game across Yorkshire. Their work includes:

- **Club support** – Helping local cricket clubs with funding, facilities, safeguarding, and governance. (County boards implement safeguarding policies set by the ECB, ensuring all clubs meet national standards.)

- **Coaching and education** – Running coach education courses, umpiring programmes, and school cricket initiatives.

- **Participation and inclusion** – Ensuring cricket is accessible to all, including programmes for women and girls, disability cricket, and community outreach.

---

[3] The Yorkshire Cricket Board and Yorkshire Cricket Foundation merged in July 2025 becoming The Yorkshire Cricket Foundation (YCF)

- **Talent pathways** – Identifying talented young players and linking them into county academies.

- **Competitions** – Organising leagues, county age-group cricket, and recreational tournaments.

Think of it like this: county clubs are the professional shop window, while county boards are the grassroots foundation, together they form the structure of cricket in England.

Why They Matter

This system ensures there's a clear pathway from village green to international stage:

In counties with separate boards, the pathway runs:
Local club → County board programme → County academy → County first XI → England.

In counties with merged structures, players move directly from club cricket into the county's pathway system.

It's a model that has produced legends from Geoffrey Boycott (Yorkshire) to Ben Stokes (Durham).

And just as important, it means cricket isn't only about producing England stars, it's about making sure thousands of people across the country, of all ages and backgrounds, can pick up a bat or ball and enjoy the game.

CHAPTER FORTY-THREE: COUNTY CRICKET CLUBS

Cricket in England and Wales has always been more than just a sport. It is a web of tradition, loyalty, and local pride, woven into the counties themselves. The county game is the backbone of English cricket: it produces England's Test players, but just as importantly, it binds communities together through leagues, schools, and village clubs. To understand modern cricket, the packed stands of The Hundred, the roar of an Ashes Test, the thrill of a T20 Blast final, we must begin with the counties who nurtured the game over centuries.

The Old Guard: Sussex, Nottinghamshire, and Kent

Sussex County Cricket Club – The Oldest of Them All

If cricket has a home in England beyond Lord's, it may well be Sussex. Formed in 1839, Sussex CCC proudly holds the title of the oldest county cricket club in the world. Yet the county's cricketing heritage stretches even further back. The first ever reference to cricket being played comes from Guildford, Surrey, in 1550, but by the early 17th century, Sussex villages such as Horsham, Arundel, and Chichester were hotbeds of the new game.

When Sussex formalised their club in the 1830s, they were led by the remarkable Sussex Martlets, a group of wealthy enthusiasts who bankrolled the game in its infancy. The great William Lillywhite and James Broadbridge, Sussex professionals, became national figures in the early 19th century, laying the groundwork for the county's future.

Over the years Sussex produced legends: C.B. Fry, who nearly captained England at football as well as cricket; Ranjitsinhji, the Indian prince whose leg-glance became one of the game's most elegant strokes; and Jim Parks, the great wicketkeeper-batsman. In the modern era, Sussex fans thrilled to the exploits of Tony Greig, Imran Khan, and more recently Chris Adams' side, who delivered three County Championships in the 2000s.

Today, Sussex continue to play at Hove, their spiritual home by the sea. The Sussex Cricket Board oversees grassroots development, women's cricket (feeding into the

Southern Vipers), and disability programmes across the South Coast. In many ways, the spirit of those early Martlets lives on in the community work that keeps cricket thriving in towns and villages.

Nottinghamshire County Cricket Club – Outlaws of the Trent

Founded in 1841, Nottinghamshire CCC's heart beats at Trent Bridge, one of cricket's most iconic grounds. From the start, Nottinghamshire built a reputation for producing fast bowlers who terrorised opposition batsmen. William Clarke, who also founded the All-England Eleven touring side, was a key early figure, and by the 1860s, the fiery quicks George Parr and John Jackson made Nottinghamshire feared across the land.

The county's golden reputation was cemented with the arrival of Arthur Shrewsbury, a masterful batsman who captained England, and the extraordinary all-rounder Richard Daft. By the 20th century, Nottinghamshire was synonymous with power players: Harold Larwood and Bill Voce, the spearheads of the infamous Bodyline series of 1932–33.

In the modern era, Clive Rice, Richard Hadlee, and Chris Cairns made Trent Bridge a fortress in the 1980s and 1990s, leading to one-day dominance. More recently, Graeme Swann, Stuart Broad, and Alex Hales carried the flag.

Off the field, the Nottinghamshire Cricket Board manages grassroots cricket across the East Midlands, focusing on youth development, women's cricket (through the Blaze regional hub), and strong disability pathways. From the Victorian tearaways of Bodyline to the modern T20 Outlaws, Nottinghamshire embodies cricket's constant capacity to adapt and thrill.

Kent County Cricket Club – Gentlemen, Players, and a Legacy of Grace

Kent is one of cricket's true heartlands. Although the county club was formally founded in 1842, cricket had been thriving in Kent for more than a century before that. Matches between 'Kent' and 'All-England' sides were recorded as early as the 1700s, often held at grounds such as Dartford Brent, Bromley Common, and the Artillery Ground in London.

The early Kent teams were studded with pioneers. In the 18th century, the Duke of Dorset was famed as both a patron and participant. By the 19th century, Kent became known for elegance and skill. Their early stars included Alfred Mynn, one of the game's first great all-rounders, and later Lord Harris, who captained England and became one of cricket's most influential administrators.

In the 20th century, Kent was the home of brilliance: Frank Woolley, with his 58,000 runs and gravity-defying catches; Colin Cowdrey, England captain and a model of batting grace; and Derek Underwood, England's greatest left-arm spinner.
Their 1970s side under Asif Iqbal was one of the most attractive teams in county cricket, winning one-day trophies galore.

The county's base at Canterbury remains steeped in tradition, with the annual Canterbury Cricket Week being the oldest festival in English cricket. The Kent Cricket Board looks after grassroots development across the county, ensuring that cricket is played in schools, villages, and towns, and that women's and girls' cricket continues to expand in the Garden of England.

Surrey County Cricket Club – The Oval and the Capital's Giants

Founded in 1845, Surrey CCC was born at the heart of the nation's capital and quickly became one of the most powerful clubs in the land. Their home, The Oval, was already a famous sporting venue, having hosted football matches, athletics, and even the first ever international Test in England (against Australia in 1880). From the moment Surrey took it on as their headquarters, it became synonymous with English cricket.

Surrey's early strength was built on batsmen of class and bowlers of great guile. The great Tom Richardson, one of the fastest bowlers of the 19th century, terrorised batsmen worldwide. In the 20th century, Surrey became truly dominant: between 1952 and 1958, under captain Stuart Surridge, they won the County Championship seven years in a row, an achievement that has never been matched.

Great names flowed through the Oval's gates: Jack Hobbs, the "Master," who scored 61,760 first-class runs and remains cricket's all-time record scorer; Alec Bedser, England's great post-war fast bowler; and more recently Alec Stewart, Graham Thorpe, Mark Butcher, and Kevin Pietersen. Today, Ollie Pope, Rory Burns, and Sam Curran carry the Surrey flag for England.

The Surrey Cricket Foundation manages grassroots cricket in one of the busiest urban environments in the world. They run youth programmes across South London, ensure inner-city cricket has opportunities to flourish, and oversee women's and disability cricket. The club remains one of the best-supported in the country, with the Oval routinely packed for T20 Blast nights.

Hampshire County Cricket Club – The Southern Tradition

Founded in 1863, Hampshire CCC is rooted in one of the cradles of cricket itself. The Hambledon Club, based in rural Hampshire in the 18th century, is often called the "birthplace of modern cricket", where the Laws of the game were refined and first codified before MCC took over that role in 1787. Hampshire CCC therefore carried a deep historical weight when it was formalised in the 19th century.

In the early years, Hampshire were not among the strongest counties, but they had iconic players like Phil Mead, a prolific batsman of the early 20th century, and Charlie Knott, a celebrated bowler. The county's modern transformation came in the 1960s and 1970s, when Barry Richards (South Africa) and Gordon Greenidge (West Indies) formed one of the most destructive opening partnerships in county history.

Hampshire's move to the Ageas Bowl (Southampton) in 2001 marked a new era. The ground is now a Test venue, hosting international cricket and The Hundred's Southern Brave franchise.

disability cricket programmes, and rural outreach. Hampshire combines the sport's deepest traditions (Hambledon) with one of its most modern stadiums.

Lancashire County Cricket Club – Roses, Legends, and Old Trafford

Founded in 1864, Lancashire CCC sits at the heart of one of English cricket's fiercest rivalries: the Roses rivalry with Yorkshire. Their base, Old Trafford in Manchester, is one of the most iconic stadiums in world cricket.

Lancashire were early powerhouses of the game, and by the late 19th century they had already established themselves as one of the best-supported counties. A.N.

Hornby, immortalised in the poem "At Lord's" after losing to Australia in 1882 (the birth of the Ashes), was one of their earliest famous captains.

The 20th century saw Lancashire blessed with a conveyor belt of stars. Cyril Washbrook, Brian Statham (England's great fast bowler), and Jack Bond's one-day side of the 1970s made Old Trafford roar. In the 1990s and early 2000s, players like Wasim Akram, Muttiah Muralitharan, and Andrew Flintoff brought global fame. Flintoff, in particular, became a folk hero in England's 2005 Ashes triumph.

Today, Lancashire continue to be major players in the Championship and the T20 Blast, where their team, the Lancashire Lightning, are among the strongest. Old Trafford remains a favourite international venue, known for its lively atmosphere.

The Lancashire Cricket Board runs grassroots programmes across Greater Manchester, Merseyside, and beyond. They manage one of the biggest junior systems in the country, extensive women's and girls' cricket, and thriving disability cricket pathways. In communities across the North West, from urban Manchester to rural Cumbria, cricket is sustained by Lancashire's broad reach.

Middlesex County Cricket Club – Lord's Own County

Formed in 1864, Middlesex CCC has the unique distinction of calling Lord's Cricket Ground its home, the self-styled "Home of Cricket." Though cricket in Middlesex goes back to the 18th century, the county club formalised just as the sport was accelerating into professionalism.

Middlesex quickly became one of the most stylish sides in the game. In the late 19th century, W.G. Grace himself turned out for them on occasion, though his heart lay in Gloucestershire. The early stars included Pelham Warner, who captained England and later became one of the game's great administrators.

The interwar years brought Patsy Hendren, a flamboyant batsman who scored over 57,000 first-class runs, and Gubby Allen, a dashing fast bowler. After WWII, Middlesex sides often bristled with class. Denis Compton, the "Brylcreem Boy," lit up the 1940s with his dashing strokes, while Mike Brearley, England's cerebral Ashes-winning captain, brought tactical nous in the 1970s.

Middlesex have remained a force into the modern era, with players like Andrew Strauss, Angus Fraser, and Phil Tufnell carrying the county's flag. Today, Middlesex remain strong in the Championship and feed talent into England via Lord's, a ground that symbolises the heart of the game.

The Middlesex Cricket Board plays a vital role in London's grassroots scene: developing cricket in schools, managing youth leagues, supporting women's and disability cricket, and ensuring the capital remains a hotbed of the game.

Derbyshire County Cricket Club – The Miners' County

Derbyshire CCC, founded in 1870, were among the first wave of northern counties to join the Championship. Their home at the County Ground, Derby, became a bastion of cricket for the East Midlands, representing a county proud of its mining and working-class heritage.

In their early years, Derbyshire often struggled to compete with richer counties, but they produced some hardy cricketers. William Mycroft, a left-arm fast bowler of the 1870s, took more than 800 wickets and was feared by batsmen everywhere.

The county's greatest triumph came in 1936, when Derbyshire won their only County Championship, under the captaincy of Arthur Richardson, with Bill Copson and Tommy Mitchell spearheading a deadly bowling attack.

Derbyshire have had their moments in one-day cricket too, winning the NatWest Trophy in 1981. Later players like Kim Barnett, a prolific run-scorer, and Dominic Cork, an England all-rounder, gave the county a proud identity.

The Derbyshire Cricket Board today oversees grassroots cricket across a county where football and rugby are strong competitors. They manage youth and women's cricket, community initiatives, and outreach projects to ensure cricket survives and thrives in Derbyshire towns and villages.

Gloucestershire County Cricket Club – The House That Grace Built

If Yorkshire is defined by Sutcliffe and Hutton, Gloucestershire will forever be defined by one man: W.G. Grace. Founded in 1870, Gloucestershire CCC quickly became famous thanks to the extraordinary feats of the Grace family. W.G. Grace, his brothers E.M. and Fred, and a host of talented amateurs built the county into one of the strongest sides of the late 19th century.

Grace himself was more than a cricketer: he was a phenomenon. With his massive beard and booming personality, he made cricket a national sport. He scored over 54,000 first-class runs, took more than 2,800 wickets, and became the face of the Victorian game. Gloucestershire, playing at Bristol, became his kingdom.

After Grace's era, Gloucestershire retained a reputation for style and skill. Charlie Townsend, Gilbert Jessop (nicknamed "The Croucher" for his hitting), and later Wally Hammond, one of England's greatest batsmen, made the county formidable.

The 1970s saw a new golden era with Mike Procter, the South African all-rounder who dominated county cricket, and later one-day masters like Jack Russell and David "Syd" Lawrence.

Gloucestershire were giants of limited-overs cricket in the late 1990s and early 2000s, winning multiple one-day trophies under captain Mark Alleyne and coach John Bracewell.

Today, the Gloucestershire Cricket Board manages grassroots cricket across the West Country, with strong ties to the South West women's pathway feeding into the Western Storm. They remain one of the most colourful counties, forever linked with the bearded genius of Grace.

Worcestershire County Cricket Club – Pears by the Severn

Worcestershire CCC, founded in 1865, is affectionately known as the "Pears," a nod to the county's famous emblem. Their home ground, New Road, Worcester, is one of the most picturesque in English cricket, lying alongside the River Severn. Floods have regularly washed across the outfield, yet the ground remains beloved by players and fans alike.

Worcestershire rose to prominence in the early 20th century but enjoyed their true golden era much later, in the 1960s and 1970s. The great Basil D'Oliveira, who had fled apartheid South Africa, made his home here and became a symbol of cricket's role in breaking down barriers. His selection for England in 1968 triggered the infamous "D'Oliveira Affair," which reshaped international cricket's stance on South Africa.

The county's finest years came in the 1980s, when they twice won the County Championship (1988 and 1989), powered by the great batting of Graeme Hick, one of county cricket's most prolific run-scorers. Ian Botham also played out his later years at New Road, adding to the club's legend.

Today, Worcestershire remain proud participants in all formats, with their T20 side, the Worcestershire Rapids, winning the Vitality Blast in 2018.

The Worcestershire Cricket Board oversees grassroots cricket in a small but passionate county, focusing on youth development, schools, and women's cricket, ensuring the game continues to thrive by the Severn.

Warwickshire County Cricket Club – The Bears of Birmingham

Warwickshire CCC was founded in 1882, relatively late compared to many counties, but their rise was swift. Their headquarters at Edgbaston, Birmingham, has become one of England's premier cricket grounds, a fortress for both county and country.

The county's early fortunes were lifted by the arrival of Frank Foster and Sydney Barnes, the latter one of England's greatest bowlers, who inspired Warwickshire to their first Championship in 1911.

The post-war years brought stability, but it was in the 1990s that Warwickshire exploded into greatness. Under the captaincy of Dermot Reeve and later Brian Lara, Warwickshire won three trophies in 1994, including the Championship, NatWest Trophy, and Sunday League. That summer, Lara scored his famous 501 not out against Durham at Edgbaston, the highest score in first-class cricket history.

Other greats include Bob Willis, the fiery fast bowler who led England to Ashes glory in 1981, and Jonathan Trott, the calm run-machine of the 2000s.

Warwickshire's modern T20 side, the Birmingham Bears, remain competitive, while Edgbaston regularly hosts Tests, ODIs, and T20Is, famous for its raucous atmosphere.

The Warwickshire Cricket Board manages a huge grassroots network across Birmingham and the West Midlands, driving participation in schools, youth, women's, and disability cricket. Their community programmes also use cricket to build cohesion in one of England's most diverse cities.

Leicestershire County Cricket Club – The Foxes of Grace Road

Founded in 1879, Leicestershire CCC are known as the "Foxes," after the county emblem. Their home at Grace Road, Leicester has been their base for over a century.

Leicestershire's early years were modest, and for much of their history they have been seen as underdogs. Yet they have consistently punched above their weight, especially in limited-overs cricket.

The county produced players of immense character: Charles Palmer, an England batsman and captain in the 1950s; Jack Birkenshaw, a fine all-rounder; and later David Gower, one of England's most elegant left-handers. Gower's cover drive became a symbol of grace itself.

The 1990s and early 2000s saw Leicestershire excel in the shortest format. They won the T20 Blast in 2004, 2006, and 2011, making them one of the competition's most successful counties. Players like Darren Maddy, a T20 pioneer, and Paul Nixon, the irrepressible wicketkeeper, gave them a giant-killing reputation.

The Leicestershire Cricket Board works hard to promote grassroots cricket in a county with diverse communities. They run youth programmes, women's and girls' cricket, and have invested heavily in engaging South Asian communities in Leicester, making cricket a vital cultural link in the city.

Essex County Cricket Club – East End Spirit

Essex CCC was founded in 1876 and became a first-class county in 1894. Based at Chelmsford, Essex has always carried a certain grit and underdog spirit, drawing support from the East End of London out into the fields of East Anglia.

For decades Essex was regarded as plucky but unsuccessful, struggling to compete with richer counties. But the 1970s and 1980s saw their golden era under Keith Fletcher and Graham Gooch. Gooch, one of England's greatest ever batsmen, led Essex to six County Championships between 1979 and 1992, transforming their reputation.

Other stars followed: Nasser Hussain, who became England captain at the turn of the millennium; Alastair Cook, England's highest-ever Test run-scorer; and bowlers like Neil Foster and Derek Pringle. In the modern era, Essex have thrived again, winning the Championship in 2017 and 2019, powered by the runs of Sir Alastair Cook and the wickets of Simon Harmer.

The Essex Cricket Board oversees cricket across one of England's most populous counties, promoting youth cricket in schools, running strong women's and girls' programmes, and supporting urban cricket initiatives in East London.

Somerset County Cricket Club – Fierce Independence in the West

Somerset CCC was founded in 1875 and became a first-class county in 1891. The club has always been fiercely proud of its independence and strong local support. Their home ground, Taunton, is one of the most atmospheric in the country, with packed stands and cider-fuelled fans giving the county a unique identity.

For much of their early history, Somerset struggled, but they were rich in character. The county produced Lionel Palairet and Sammy Woods in the early 20th century, but true glory came in the late 1970s and early 1980s, when Somerset had one of the greatest one-day teams in history.

With Ian Botham, Viv Richards, and Joel Garner all playing together, Somerset were unstoppable, winning five one-day trophies between 1979 and 1983. Though they have never won the County Championship, their loyal fans have cherished one-day triumphs and near-misses in red-ball cricket.

Modern heroes include Marcus Trescothick, a beloved opener who became one of England's finest batsmen, and Jack Leach, the folk hero of the 2019 Ashes at Headingley.

The Somerset Cricket Board works tirelessly in a rural county to promote youth and schools' cricket, with an emphasis on women's and girls' pathways feeding into the Western Storm. The club's strong community ties make Taunton one of English cricket's best-loved venues.

Northamptonshire County Cricket Club – Late Bloomers, Big Punch

Northamptonshire CCC was founded in 1878 and became a first-class county in 1905, making them one of the later entrants to the Championship. Known as "Northants" or the "Steelbacks" in modern limited-overs cricket, they play at the County Ground, Northampton.

Northants struggled for much of their early history, often finishing near the bottom of the table. Yet they have produced outstanding cricketers: George Thompson, a fine all-rounder in the early 20th century; Dennis Brookes, a stalwart batsman of the mid-century; and later Colin Milburn, a swashbuckling batsman whose career was tragically curtailed by a car accident.

Though Championship glory has eluded them, Northants have been excellent in one-day formats. They won the NatWest Trophy in 1992 and became one of the most consistent T20 sides in the 2010s, winning the T20 Blast in 2013 and 2016.

Today, Northants remain competitive, with a reputation for team spirit and shrewd recruitment. The Northamptonshire Cricket Board ensures cricket thrives in one of England's smaller counties, focusing on schools, women's development, and disability cricket.

Yorkshire County Cricket Club – The White Rose Giants

No county dominates cricket's history quite like Yorkshire CCC, founded in 1863. Based at Headingley, Leeds, Yorkshire has been the most successful county in Championship history, winning the title 33 times outright and sharing it twice.

Yorkshire's identity has always been bound up with pride, tradition, and a fierce sense of place. Until the 1990s, the club even had a rule that only players born within the county could represent them. This produced generations of world-class cricketers who embodied the county's values.

The list of Yorkshire legends is staggering: Wilfred Rhodes, who played a record 1,110 first-class matches; Herbert Sutcliffe and Len Hutton, two of England's greatest ever opening batsmen; Fred Trueman, the fiery fast bowler with over 300 Test wickets; and later Geoffrey Boycott, whose stubborn, determined batting summed up the Yorkshire ethos.

In the modern era, players like Michael Vaughan, Joe Root, and Jonny Bairstow have carried the White Rose into the international stage. Root, in particular, has become one of England's greatest batsmen.

The Yorkshire Cricket Board (YCB)[4] oversees grassroots cricket across England's largest county, from village pitches in the Dales to bustling inner-city clubs in Leeds, Bradford, and Sheffield. They run youth programmes, women's cricket pathways feeding into the Northern Diamonds, and disability teams, ensuring Yorkshire remains the beating heart of English cricket.

Glamorgan County Cricket Club – Pride of Wales

Glamorgan CCC, founded in 1888, became a first-class county in 1921, making them the only Welsh club in the County Championship. Based primarily at Sophia Gardens, Cardiff (now the SWALEC Stadium), Glamorgan embody Welsh cricketing pride.

Glamorgan's greatest triumphs came in the Championship, which they won in 1948, 1969, and 1997. The 1948 title was led by Wilf Wooller, an inspirational all-rounder, while the 1969 side featured Majid Khan, the elegant Pakistani batsman. In 1997, captained by Matthew Maynard and powered by Steve Watkin's bowling, Glamorgan stunned bigger counties to win again.

Glamorgan have also produced and hosted international stars, including Robert Croft, Simon Jones (2005 Ashes winner), and South Africans like Jacques Rudolph. Sophia Gardens is now a regular international venue, hosting Tests and limited overs matches, including the 2019 World Cup.

The Cricket Wales Board works alongside Glamorgan to grow the game across Wales. They promote school cricket in rural areas, women's and girls' cricket, and community outreach in Cardiff, Swansea, and the Valleys. Glamorgan remain the flagbearer for Welsh cricket.

---

[4] The Yorkshire Cricket Board and Yorkshire Cricket Foundation merged in July 2025 becoming The Yorkshire Cricket Foundation (YCF)

Durham County Cricket Club – The Modern Era's Bold Newcomer

Durham CCC was founded in 1882, but only joined the first-class county ranks in 1992, making them the newest of the 18 major counties. Their rise was a statement: cricket needed to grow in the North East, and Durham were determined to prove they belonged.

Based at Chester-le-Street (Riverside Ground), Durham quickly became a powerhouse. In less than 20 years, they won the County Championship three times (2008, 2009, 2013), built on the brilliance of Steve Harmison, Paul Collingwood, and later Ben Stokes, one of the greatest all-rounders in the world today.

Durham's success story is remarkable: from outsiders to champions, and from no Test ground to hosting Ashes cricket at Riverside in 2013. They have also been a cradle for England fast bowlers, producing Harmison, Graham Onions, and Mark Wood.

The Durham Cricket Board oversees development across the North East, an area where cricket historically competed with football for attention. They run youth leagues, women's programmes feeding into the Northern Diamonds, and community cricket in cities like Newcastle, Sunderland, and Durham.

THE ENDLESS STORY OF CRICKET

Cricket's story is not simply one of a sport, but of people, places, and passions woven together across centuries. From shepherd boys knocking stones with sticks on English commons, to floodlit stadiums hosting millions of viewers worldwide, the game has travelled an extraordinary distance.

At its heart, cricket has always been about balance, between bat and ball, attack and defence, patience and daring. It is a contest that can last for a single over or stretch for five days, yet its essence remains the same. Whether it is a tense Test match at Lord's, a high-scoring IPL clash in Mumbai, or a Sunday league game on a Yorkshire village green, cricket speaks the same language of skill, strategy, and spirit.

The game has never stood still. Each century brought its own revolution: the codifying of the Laws in the 18th century, the rise of county cricket in the 19th, the explosion of international contests and superstar players in the 20th, and the arrival of T20s and global franchise leagues in the 21st. Today, innovations such as The Hundred and cricket's return to the Olympics show that the sport continues to adapt without losing sight of its traditions.

Just as important is the way cricket reflects the world around it. Once bound up in empire, it became a means for nations to assert independence and pride. Once dominated by class divisions, it grew into a professional sport open to all backgrounds. Once seen as a male preserve, it is now being reshaped by women's cricket, with record crowds, prime-time coverage, and role models inspiring a new generation of players.

Cricket's endurance lies in its contradictions: a game both timeless and modern, intensely local yet global, slow and thoughtful yet capable of explosive brilliance. It is a sport where legends are born Grace, Bradman, Sobers, Tendulkar, Perry, Stokes yet it still belongs to every child who picks up a bat or bowls their first ball on a patch of grass.

As this book has shown, cricket is more than scores and statistics. It is the roar of the Barmy Army, the quiet dignity of groundstaff working through the night, the hush before a bowler steams in, and the eruption of joy when bat meets ball. It is the traditions of county cricket and the innovations of T20. It is history, heritage, and hope, all carried on the seam of a ball.

And the story is still being written. Every match adds another layer, every player another chapter, every fan another voice in the chorus. Cricket is not finished, nor will it ever be because as long as a ball can be bowled and a bat can be swung, the game will carry on, endlessly fascinating, endlessly changing, endlessly loved.

Acknowledgements

My heartfelt thanks go to Beryl Sanderson, who also came to cricket later in life and is now taking her own coaching course in November 2025. Thank you for being the first to read this book, for checking it so carefully and for your honest and helpful feedback.

I am grateful to Lorna Upton for going through the manuscript with her official cricket rule book beside her, checking for accuracy.

My thanks also go to Stephen Towler, a lifelong cricket fan, for proofreading the text and offering valuable formatting suggestions that strengthened many chapters.

Finally, I would like to thank Louise Ellis Jones for working through the first ten chapters with a fine tooth comb and helping to shape the final version.

I am eternally grateful to you all.

Bibliography & References

Official Laws and Governing Bodies

Marylebone Cricket Club (MCC). *The Laws of Cricket*. Latest ed., MCC, London.
International Cricket Council (ICC). *ICC Playing Conditions* (Tests, ODIs, T20Is). ICC, Dubai.
England and Wales Cricket Board (ECB). *ECB Regulations and Competition Rules*. ECB, London.

Historical Works on Cricket

Altham, H. S. *A History of Cricket*. George Allen & Unwin.
Birley, Derek. *A Social History of English Cricket*. Aurum Press.
Barclay, J. *Barclay's World of Cricket*. Collins.
Box, Charles. *Cricket: Its History and Its Heroes*. London, 1868.
Brodribb, Gerald. *The History of Cricket: From the Weald to the World*. Lennard Publishing.
Underdown, David. *Start of Play: Cricket and Culture in Eighteenth-Century England*. Allen Lane.
Webber, Roy. *Phoenix History of Cricket*. Phoenix House.

County & Domestic Cricket

ACS (Association of Cricket Statisticians and Historians). *A Guide to First-Class Cricket*. ACS Publications.
Gibson, Alan. *The County Game*. Pelham Books.
Wisden. *Wisden Cricketers' Almanack*. Annual editions.

Biographies & Autobiographies

Grace, W. G. *Cricketing Reminiscences*.
Bradman, Don. *Farewell to Cricket*.
Botham, Ian. *Botham: My Autobiography*.
Boycott, Geoffrey. *Boycs: The Autobiography*.
Flintoff, Andrew. *Being Freddie*.
Perry, Ellyse. *Perspective*.
Knight, Heather. Various interviews and articles.

Women's Cricket

Rapoport, Amy, and Hart, G. *Fair Play: The Story of Women's Cricket.*
Wilson, Rachael. *Pioneers of the Women's Game.*
ECB. *Women's Cricket Pathway & Regulations.*

Disability Cricket

Lord's Taverners. *Table Cricket & Disability Cricket Programmes.*
ECB. *Disability Cricket Pathway Guidance.*
Blind Cricket England & Wales. Official rules and historical documents.

Match Records & Statistics

ESPNcricinfo. *StatsGuru Database.*
CricketArchive. *Match and Player Records.*
Wisden Online & Print Almanacks.
Playfair Cricket Annual.

Equipment History

MCC Museum. *Cricket Artefacts Collection.*
Gunn & Moore. *GM Batmaking Archives.*
Gray-Nicolls. *History of the Cricket Bat.*
Duke & Son. *Manufacturing Notes and Ball Specifications.*

Formats (T20, The Hundred, WTC)

Bose, Mihir. *The Story of the T20 Revolution.*
Sharma, Suresh. *The IPL Phenomenon.*
ECB. *The Hundred: Competition Playing Conditions.*
ICC. *World Test Championship Documentation.*

Grounds & Institutions

Lord's Cricket Ground. MCC Archives and Museum Notes.
The Oval (Surrey CCC). Club historical material.
Edgbaston (Warwickshire CCC). Club records and archives.
Trent Bridge (Nottinghamshire CCC). Club publications.

Reputable News & Feature Sources

BBC Sport Cricket.
The Guardian. Cricket coverage and long reads.

The Telegraph Sport.
The Times Cricket Section.
CricBuzz.

FURTHER READING

Marylebone Cricket Club. *The Laws of Cricket, 2017 Code (latest edition)*. Lord's Cricket Ground, London.

Wisden Cricketers' Almanack. Annual reference work. Bloomsbury Publishing.

England and Wales Cricket Board. *Introducing Cricket: Coaching and Participation Resources*. ECB, London. (Including All Stars and Dynamos programme materials.)

Birley, Derek. *A Social History of English Cricket*. Aurum Press.

Frindall, Bill (ed.). *The Wisden Book of Cricket Records*. Headline.

Barclay, Gordon (ed.). *Barclay's World of Cricket: The Game from A–Z*. Collins.

Nicholson, Rafaelle. *Ladies and Lords: A History of Women's Cricket in Britain*. (History Press.)

International Cricket Council. *Playing Conditions and Regulations* and historical overviews at the ICC official website.

Lord's Taverners. Materials and reports on disability and inclusive cricket.

Blind Cricket England and Wales; England and Wales Cricket Board Disability Cricket pages; and national disability cricket bodies for background on blind, deaf and disability cricket programmes.

www.ingramcontent.com/pod-product-compliance
Lightning Source LLC
Chambersburg PA
CBHW040326100526
44584CB00002BA/131